RELATEDNESS

RELATEDNESS

Essays in Metaphysics and Theology

Harold H. Oliver
Boston University

MERCER

ISBN 0-86554-141-8

All books published by Mercer University Press are produced
on acid-free paper that exceeds the minimum standards set by
the National Historical Publications and Records Commission.

Library of Congress Cataloging in Publication Data
Oliver, Harold H.
    Relatedness : essays in metaphysics and theology
    Bibliography: p. 175.
    Includes index.
    1. Philosophical theology—Addresses, essays,
lectures.   2. Hermeneutics—Addresses, essays, lectures.
I. Title.
BT40.044   1984   230   84-1152
ISBN 0-86554-141-8 (alk. paper)

Contents

To
Prof. Dr. Christos S. Voulgaris
Καθηγητῇ τοῦ Πανεπιστημίου ᾿Αθηνῶν
with esteem and affection

Acknowledgments

The author would like to thank:

The Joint Publication Board of Zygon, and its present editor, Dr. Karl E. Peters, for permission to reprint the article, "The Complementarity of Theology and Cosmology," *Zygon: Journal of Religion and Science* 13:1 (March 1978): 19-33;

The Theological Faculty of the University of Basel, and the current Redaktion, Prof. Dr. Klaus Seybold, for permission to reprint the article, "Theses on the Relational Self and the Genesis of the Western Ego," *Theologische Zeitschrift* (Basel) 33 (November 1977): 326-35;

The University of Notre Dame Press, and its editor, Dr. James R. Langford; and Dr. Leroy S. Rouner, director of The Boston University Institute for Philosophy and Religion, for permission to reprint the article, "Relational Ontology and Hermeneutics," that appeared originally in *Myth, Symbol and Reality*, ed. Alan M. Olson, Boston University Studies in Philosophy and Religion 1 (Notre

Dame and London: University of Notre Dame Press, 1980) 69-85; and

Professor Ross Fitzgerald and Pergamon Press (Australia) Pty. Ltd., for permission to reprint the article, "Relational Metaphysics and the Human Future," that appeared in *The Sources of Hope,* ed. Ross Fitzgerald (Pergamon Press [Australia] Pty. Ltd., 1979) 176-97.

The article, "A Relational Reassessment of Myth," first appeared in *Nexus* (54 [1977]: 11-18), the alumni/ae publication of the Boston University School of Theology. Acknowledgment is made to the dean, Dr. Richard D. Nesmith, and the faculty, and especially to the librarian, Prof. William E. Zimpfer, who served as editor at that time.

The author wishes to thank his former student, Dr. Karl Squier of Winchester, and his graduate assistant, Sr. Jeanne Gallo, SND, for valuable editorial assistance in the final preparation of the manuscript.

Funds for the preparation of the manuscript were graciously provided by The School of Theology and The Graduate School of Arts and Sciences of Boston University. For this important support I wish to thank Dean Nesmith and Dr. Michael Mendillo, associate dean of The Graduate School.

Finally, gratitude is expressed to Mercer University Press for encouragement and support.

Harold H. Oliver
Boston University

Introduction

One of the clearest omens that we may be entering a post-Enlightenment age is the current obsession with wholeness, that is, with holistic as opposed to analytic representations of reality. Even the recent preoccupation with secularity seems to be receding before the realization that the notion of the "world come of age" may represent, not the vindication of the Enlightenment, but its dénouement. "One-eyed reason"[1] is rapidly losing its appeal among those who experience the added dimension of binocular Vision.

The most serious crisis of our time is conceptual and cultural. Established conceptualities are proving inadequate to interpret the deeper Vision of experience associated with the new interactions between diverse cultures. To the extent that every culture represents a conceptual structuring of a society, cultural crises call for conceptual reformations. If such cultural reformations are to be

---

[1]Alfred North Whitehead, *Science and the Modern World, Lowell Lectures 1925* (New York: The Free Press, 1967; first published in 1925) 59.

worthy successors of their antecedents, they must arise out of discernment as to the precise nature of the conceptual predicament and must be attended by some pre-Vision of hitherto neglected conceptualities of greater promise. The re-Vision of culture requires a more adequate en-Visioning of its possibilities.

The essays in this volume begin with a reexamination of the conceptual foundations of modern Western culture and culminate in a proposal for radical revisions of our fundamental notions. My intention is not to add to the dilemma of modernity, but to aid those who share my conviction that the most serious intellectual task of our time is a reasoned and passionate reaccessing of modernity. The established texture of modern Western culture represents choices made wittingly or unwittingly by persons of influence; nothing is more pressing today than an unraveling of the threads of thought and value which are woven into the fabric of our culture through these choices. Progress in this task could transform the burden of the past—and it is a present burden—into a blessing.

The ten essays in this volume represent the extension of a programmatic work on metaphysics published in 1981, but virtually completed in manuscript form in the mid-1970s.[2] Five of the essays appear in print here for the first time. The ten essays are arranged in the order in which they were written so as to exhibit the way in which the ideas evolved.

The first essay provides an opportunity to place the thesis of the complementarity of theology and cosmology advanced in the book[3] into the wider context of the debate about "complementarity."

The second esssay develops the hermeneutical suggestions made in the book[4] in the direction of a more substantial theory of

---

[2]Harold H. Oliver, *A Relational Metaphysic*, Studies in Philosophy and Religion 4 (The Hague: Martinus Nijhoff Publishers, 1981).

[3]Ibid., 151-75.

[4]Ibid., 182-84.

text interpretation which is further expanded in essays 4, 7, 8, and 9.

When Fritz Buri, my sometime mentor in Basel, suggested to me the relevance of the writings of Nishida Kitaro for the program I had set for myself, I realized the need to give deeper thought to the notion of relational selfhood which I had proposed in the book manuscript.[5] A comparison of Nishida's notion of Pure Experience with cognate notions in Zen and in the writings of Meister Eckhart broadened the base of my notion of the relational self. Essay 3, written appropriately for the Buri Festschrift issue of *Theologische Zeitschrift*, represents an enrichment of the concept of relational selfhood brought about by greater dependence on the notions of Pure Experience and Immediacy.

Essay 4 returns to the theme of hermeneutics. New in this essay is the realization on my part that historicism had been so determinative for hermeneutics. This initial critique of historicism is expanded in essays 7 and 9. Evident also is a realization of a greater affinity with the hermeneutical theory of Hans-Georg Gadamer.

Neither the book-manuscript nor subsequent essays focused attention on the ethical implications of my relational conception of experience. My attempt in essay 5 to address this question was aided by insights from Nishida and Krister Stendahl. The notion of temporality hinted at in the book-manuscript[6] became the vital clue for my formulation of a relational reassessment of morality, though I did not begin a serious rethinking of temporality until essays 6 and 7. The former sets forth a phenomenology of futurity; the latter, of pastness. These essays claim that "the Past" and "the Future" are reifications arising out of nonrelational modes of thought.

Essay 7 was written as a kind of Nietzschean condemnation of the idolization of historicism that has been so characteristic of Western scholarship since the Enlightenment. My misgivings about the

---

[5]Ibid., 161-63, 179-81.

[6]Ibid., 175ff.

prevailing interpretation of David Friedrich Strauss led me to re-think his intention and subsequently to dissociate it from the historicism he has customarily been thought to have espoused at the outset of his career.

Although essay 8 also deals with hermeneutics, it is admittedly a kind of *Gedankenexperiment* enacted to test the notion, incipiently represented in essay 5, that interpretation is largely an aesthetic affair.[7] The claim is advanced that classic texts attain their eminence through their power to generate congruent meanings. If this claim is sustained, the notion of the "morality of historical knowlege" may lose whatever residual attraction it now has for some.

Essay 9, delivered as a lecture at the "First Meeting at Philippi" in Kavala, Greece, in 1980, is a refinement of the hermeneutical reassessment of historicism set forth in essay 7. Essay 9 proposes an approach to "historical" (that is, narrative) texts of eminent literature radically different from the standard historicist methodology. The Book of Acts in the New Testament is utilized to illustrate the difficulties of historicism as well as the hermeneutical possibilities of a relational approach.

The final essay in this collection returns to the themes of relational selfhood featured in essay 3. It was a lecture delivered to the Theological Faculty of The University of Athens, Greece, in 1981. It attempts to expand the suggestion first put forward in essay 5, that the notion of experience in Eastern Orthodoxy profoundly differs from prevailing notions in the Augustinian West. My intention was to supplement the claims about self-denial first made in essay 3 by attempting a more comprehensive statement about the nature of relational theology. Earlier I had highlighted Meister Eckhart's notion of "poverty in spirit" as the purest example of the notion of relational selfhood available in Western Christianity. In this final essay I argue that, while Eckhart represents the deepest understanding of the "kenotic" Christology championed in the West, his understanding did not attain to the spiritual heights of the Eastern

---

[7]Cf. esp. 57-58 in this collection.

Orthodox view of selfhood. In the latter, "kenotic" Christology is complemented by a more complete "anastasial" Christology which defines the deep structure of Eastern Orthodox spirituality and, *ipso facto*, its distinctive sense of experience.

This overview of the thematic development which unfolded during a six-year period is offered in the hope that it will reveal the relative place of each essay within the whole as well as the holistic perspective seeking coherent articulation throughout this undertaking. The present opportunity to reissue the previously published essays (1, 2, 3, 4, and 6) in the context of a more complete corpus has been utilized to bring greater coherence into the work. Although I was clear in my own mind from the outset that the "relational self" is to be distinguished from the "subject self," I was not sufficiently careful early on to communicate my intention. I have revised the text of essay 3 to preserve my intention.

The fact that the essays were written for different audiences accounts for the reiteration of fundamental terms and assumptions through successive essays. It is anticipated that such reiteration will have the redeeming effect of making my intention more lucid.

It is my hope that the present volume of essays will prove to be sufficiently self-contained to be intelligible to those who may not have read my book, *A Relational Metaphysic*, and additionally significant to those who may wish to think through its implications along lines which have subsequently occurred to me.

1 | The Complementarity of Theology and Cosmology

The title of this essay, "The Complementarity of Theology and Cosmology," juxtaposes three terms whose meanings are not self-evident; thus the claim it makes is subject to misunderstanding. The danger of poorly defined terms in such a claim is either that one will agree too readily with it, where in fact differences are real and deep, or that those who agree on the state of affairs may seem to be in disagreement. Where there is general agreement on definitions—and such a consensus is a requisite for intelligent discourse—a different set of problems arises. Either the theologian may seem to be conceding too much to the cosmologist, thereby surrendering the distinctiveness of religious claims, or the cosmologist may seem to have abandoned the scientific rigor of his profession which has been achieved in a hard-fought struggle against religious authoritarianism. Two tasks emerge from the outset: to seek to achieve some agreement on the meaning of the terms "complementarity," "theology," and "cosmology" and to defend the claim that is made by their juxtaposition.

The terminological question is complex, as a preliminary survey will indicate. The term "complementarity" took on special significance when Niels Bohr conscripted it to resolve the wave-particle paradox in quantum physics. Today there are purists who maintain that only the meaning implied in Bohr's use of the term is legitimate when applying it to a broader range of issues, while others believe—with Humpty Dumpty in *Through the Looking Glass*—that it can mean just what they choose it to mean. As I shall attempt to argue in due course, the purists are unduly rigid—as is always the case with purists—and the view of Humpty Dumpty is unduly libertine. The word "complementarity," like the terms "theology" and "cosmology," imposes some limitations on its use, and I shall try to respect these limits.

The term "theology" signifies a quasi-philosophical enterprise which has as its first item of agenda the necessity to define what it is. A consequence of this state of affairs is that there is a long and mostly illustrious history of diverse answers. Some theologians do not distinguish sharply between "religion" and "theology," believing that they represent points on a spectrum which moves more or less in a continuum from simple to formal reflection. This is my own position. Other theologians make a rigid distinction between primary religious experience and the secondary reflection upon it which is properly called "theology." The latter often further subdivide theology into second- and third-order reflection, reserving the term "metatheology" for whatever they determine to be the final stage of reflection. Although the term "theology" seems only to impose the formal restriction on the user that his reasoning be about *theos*, there is wide disagreement upon just what *theos* must mean. Some theologians claim to be focusing on religious statements, others on religious experiences, while still others hold adamantly to the view that theology is necessarily about a divine object. This scholarly pluralism reflects the general pluralism of our Judeo-Christian culture.

The term "cosmology" is equally ambiguous. Having developed at a time when physics was a branch of metaphysics, it continued for centuries to denote the science of the totality of physical reality. The separation of physics from metaphysics, which some argue was essential to the development of modern science, resulted in the eventual restriction of the term to its use in the physical sciences. The eclipse of metaphysics which attended the era of positivism in philosophy coincided with the origins of modern physical cosmology and thus set the stage for the final reduction of the term "cosmology" to the simple meaning: that branch of physics which studies the large-scale structure of the universe and its *arche* and *telos* in theories in which evolution is assumed. It must be admitted by reasonable persons, however, that there are fundamental metaphysical questions surrounding such a restriction of the term. There are in fact some philosophers, like Alfred North Whitehead, for whom cosmology is a metaphysical undertaking of the greatest comprehensiveness; Whitehead's *Process and Reality*, which represents the most nearly complete statement of his views on man, world, and God, carried the subtitle, *An Essay in Cosmology*. Other philosophers, perhaps more modestly but with no less conviction, have wished to capture the term as a designation of the total philosophical enterprise. Such is the case with Karl R. Popper who claimed, in his famous work *The Logic of Scientific Discovery*, that, *contra* the language philosophers, there is "at least one philosophical problem in which all thinking men are interested," namely, "the problem of cosmology: the problem of understanding the world—including ourselves, and our knowledge, as part of the world. All science is cosmology, I believe, and for me the interest of philosophy, no less than science, lies solely in the contribution which it has made to it."[1] However one may feel about these two positions, there is a resurgence of interest in metaphysics which may well lead to a broadening of the scope of the term cosmology and to a more concerted cooperative labor of scientists and philosophers on a purely deductive cosmology.

---

[1]Karl R. Popper, *The Logic of Scientific Discovery*, rev. ed. (London: Hutchinson, 1968) 15.

I have chosen as a means of defining the principal terms of my title to discuss first of all the major models of interaction between science and religion which hitherto have seemed viable and to use this as a *modus operandi* for suggesting a new foundation for the thesis of complementarity.

Models of the Relationship between Science and Religion Critically Compared

The relationship of theology and cosmology first became problematical with the pre-Socratics, for in the mythical worldviews which preceded them theology and cosmology were an identity. The pre-Socratics initiated the transformation from mythology to rational theory, with an inevitable resultant bifurcation between the stories of the gods and the explanation of the world. Only in periods of romanticism—like our own—with their open critique of objective science has the dream of their reunification been revived. Characteristically in the West the bifurcation has seemed to be in the best interests of both religion and science—of religion, whose spokesmen have resisted the efforts of some to make the scientific vision omnicompetent; of science, for the pathos of its modern origins was a direct function of religious myopia. In the claim of their complementarity to be advanced in due course I assume that the thesis of bifurcation is basic to both the *esse* and *bene esse* of religion and science, and I will attempt to ground this claim by showing that these two great human activities are rooted in quite different—though complementary—operations.

The relationship between religion and science has taken three major forms in the twentieth century: the conflict theory, the compartment theory, and the theory of complementarity.

The Conflict Theory

This theory assumes that science and religion represent alternative—we should say rival—theories about the same domain. Religious statements about the world are preferred by some believers to scientific theories, especially when they conflict. There are scientists as well who hold this theory, as is evident in the fact that they maintain that religious statements represent adolescent ideas about reality. Both groups interpret religious statements literally; they differ only on the question of whether such statements accurately represent an actual state of affairs. It is all too easy for those of us who value modernity to think that the conflict theory made its exit in the nineteenth century or earlier as one of the last vestiges of medieval superstition. We have been reminded recently that the theory is still defended even in the U.S., as for example in the recent altercation between the "creationists" and "advocates of science" in California. The pressure which the "creationists" in some instances have applied successfully to state officials to have the Genesis account of creation included in textbooks is clear evidence of the conflict theory. These "creationists" are not asking that the Genesis account of creation be taught as "religious instruction" since most of them are ardent defenders of the separation of Church and State. Rather they want the biblical account taught as an alternative to prevailing cosmological theories. Before we pass too severe a judgment on the narrowness of this position, we need to ask whether their overreaction to educational policy is totally unjustified. They are convinced that scientific theories of the origin of the world have been taught frequently as an alternative to the Genesis account, considered as obsolete science. The fact that the conflict model has been operative to some extent on both sides of the issue goes a long way toward explaining the intensity of the struggle between these two groups. I do not wish to be misunderstood; I hold firmly that the biblical account of creation is religious, not scientific instruction, and should be so judged by the courts of the land. The view of complementarity which I shall present implies, however, that it is equally myopic for scientists to regard the biblical account as bad science, for the Genesis account is not "science" at all. I suspect that the conflict theory is well entrenched and will have to be dealt with for a long time. The defense of complementarity in this essay is offered in the hope that this conflict theory will run its course sooner than later. I hope to show that two major alternatives to it, the compartment theory and the theory of complementarity, make for better science and religion.

The Compartment Theory

Athough it is common to think that the compartment theory can be stated simply, it in fact encompasses such a diverse following that some subcategories are needed to cover the actual situation. The general thesis of this position is that science and religion represent nonrival theories since they refer to different "domains." It is because different meanings are assigned to the term "domain" that the subcategories are needed. Scientists and theologians alike have identified frequently with this view, some for reasons of general tolerance alone. For whatever reasons, the prominence of the compartment theory has been partly responsible for providing scientists with sufficient Lebensraum to develop their theories. A negative consequence of this state of affairs, however, has been a laissez-faire attitude toward each other's work so that fruitful interaction cannot take place.

Only two subcategories of the compartment theory will be discussed. The first is that the domain of scientific statements is the physical world; the domain of religious statements is a spiritual realm, about whose exact nature theologians of this view do not seem to agree. Perhaps the kindest way of expressing what is meant by the domain of religious statements is that, whereas scientific statements refer to the physical world, religious statements refer to the source-and-ground of the world who sustains its processes. The neoorthodox theologians who dominated European and American theology for several decades all held some such view. Among the "second-generation" dialectical theologians, Thomas F. Torrance can be interpreted reasonably as representing a contemporary version of this theory in that he speaks of science and religion as each having radically different "objects" which they each should illumine in the same—that is, scientific—manner.[2]

A second subcategory of the compartment theory maintains that scientific and religious languages do not conflict because only the former is cognitively referential. When the theologians of this subview proceed to say how religious statements are to be interpreted, they further subdivide into at least two major schools.

Rudolf Bultmann and his followers held that religious language is to be interpreted not literally (objectively referential) but existentially, that is, anthropologically. Statements about God are to be interpreted as statements about man. The intentionality of religious discourse separates it categorically from scientific theory. It is interesting that Bultmann did maintain that cosmological elements in religious mythology were to be regarded primarily as "pre-" (that is, "un-") scientific. Bultmann held to the absolute priority of science over religion in matters of nature and absolute priority of religion over science in questions of human existence. This is clearly a compartment perspective.

For another group of theologians (and philosophers) religious discourse is fundamentally emotive or attitudinal language. In his infamous attempt to bring about "the elimination of metaphysics" A. J. Ayer grouped metaphysical and religious discourse together under the rubric of "emotive language." Accepting this judgment, R. B. Braithwaite proceeded to make the case that religious statements are nothing more than declarations of how believers intend to behave. Paul van Buren, under the influence of Braithwaite's empiricism, developed a theology in which the attitudinal perspective on religious discourse became the "secular meaning of the Gospel." One readily sees that for these thinkers there can be no conflict between scientific and religious statements; they stand in separate, "hermetically sealed" compartments.

---

[2]Thomas F. Torrance, *Theological Science* (London: Oxford University Press, 1969) 121, 125.

The compartment theory has been especially attractive to scientists since it guarantees them absolute freedom, while leaving open to some extent the question as to how religious language is to be evaluated. A change in a given scientist's personal attitude toward religious claims necessitates no modification of his professional habits and goals. Theologians who espouse the compartment theory feel comfortable to the degree that it removes the sense of threat which the relentless progress of science has posed to traditional religious claims.

Whatever its personal and professional assets, the compartment theory—in my judgment—does not comprehensively and adequately take account of the deepest insights and intentions of either physical theory or religious discourse. I must try to show that this claim is justified.

The Theory of Complementarity

The thesis of complementarity is that science and religion represent coordinate perspectives on the same domain. Ever since Bohr advanced the term "complementarity" to resolve paradoxes in microphysics, it has become increasingly popular to claim that science and religion offer complementary views of reality. But the fact that the term has meant such different things to those so using it has resulted in a kind of "mushy" consensus. One indication of the seriousness of the terminological issue is that two major philosophers felt compelled in a recent issue of *Zygon* to review the question and argue their respective opinions. One of these philosophers, Hugo Adam Bedau, sets out to establish the conditions for the legitimate use of the term "complementarity."[3] After surveying briefly the major options on the current scene, Bedau argues that of the two logical alternatives only one fulfills these conditions. He rejects the first option—"the *truth* of 'science and religion are complementary' depends on the truth of 'quantum mechanics involves comple-

---

[3]Hugo Adam Bedau, "Complementarity and the Relation between Science and Religion," *Zygon* 9 (1974): 202-24.

mentarity' "; nevertheless he argues a purist position of less stringency—"the *meaning* of 'science and religion are complementary' depends on the meaning of 'quantum mechanics involves complementarity.' "[4] His rejection of the first option is based appropriately on the insight that even if physicists should abandon the principle of complementarity in quantum mechanics the application of the term to the question of the relationship of science and religion would not be undermined. Does agreement with Bedau thus far entail agreement on his second option?

Bedau rephrases his central thesis in the following way: "the complementarity alleged in fields other than physics is all but unintellligible unless such allegations are based on an understanding of the term 'complementarity' on the model provided by Bohr's notion of complementarity in quantum physics."[5] It is fundamental to Bedau's case that since the would-be complementarist did not invent the neologism, he is obliged to follow the meaning assigned to it by Bohr. The argument continues: "Is he [the would-be complementarist] . . . to be guided by nothing more than the analogies provided by the meaning of 'complement' and cognate terms in pre-Bohr usage? If so, this resolves into the attempt to adapt the term from its use in logic, geometry, and chromatics; but there is no evidence that any would-be complementarist has had such analogies in mind."[6] I concede that the use of the term in quantum physics did stimulate its application to the science-religion question, but I reject—for reasons which I hope to make clear—his thesis that the meaning Bohr assigned to it is determinative for all later use. There is even some question as to whether the term "complementarity" is in fact Bohr's neologism; even if that were the case, *he* certainly must have been influenced by the meaning of the term "complement" in pre-Bohr usage!

Bedau's main point is that because the term "complementarity" was designed for the sole purpose of removing paradoxes in quan-

---

[4]Ibid., 206. [5]Ibid., 207. [6]Ibid.

tum physics its essence "is to be found in the way these paradoxes are removed."[7] Bedau's summary of Bohr's intention is accurate. The latter intended "complementarity" as a "restatement of the entire relationship between microobjects, relativizing their classical theoretical properties, corpuscularity/wavelikeness, to the experimental arrangements through which these microobjects are investigated."[8] It follows that a "categorical assignment of either property to a microobject—ascribing the property (for example, wavelikeness) without mention of the observations or experimental arrangement through which they are obtained—is, strictly speaking, meaningless."[9] I personally feel that Bedau goes too far when he concludes that it is simply impossible to waive the requirement that "there be some legitimate sense of paradox applicable to genuine difficulties relating science and religion."[10] He goes to great lengths to discredit most current theories of the complementarity of science and religion because they fail to prove that any genuine paradoxes are involved. The most Bedau will concede is that there is a "remote analogy" between complementarity in quantum physics and in the science-religion debate.

Bedau's purist position is challenged by D. M. MacKay, who nevertheless, shares the former's concern that the term "complementarity" has become "an omnibus name" for "a verbal relation, where no other is apparent."[11] Is there some way, he asks, to prevent complementarity from becoming "yet another fashionable escape gate from intellectual integrity in theology?"[12] Here the similarity between the two men ends, however. MacKay refuses to let complementarity in quantum physics become a "paradigm case"; for him, the term refers to a logical rather than a physical con-

---

[7]Ibid., 209.   [8]Ibid.

[9]Ibid.   [10]Ibid., 215.

[11]D. M. MacKay, " 'Complementarity' in Scientific and Religious Thinking," *Zygon* 9 (1974): 225.

[12]Ibid.

cept. It is a "kind of logical relation, distinct from and additional to traditional ones like contradiction, synonomy, or independence" and needs to be carefully considered "whenever there is doubt as to the connection between two statements."[13] Unlike some of the other theories of the relation of science and religion, the complementarist view holds that religious and scientific statements are logically dependent, that is, they are about the same situation. This claim leads MacKay to formulate the following strict condition for all complementary statements: that the alteration or absence of one of the statements would necessitate a change in the other. He adds the additional restriction that the "blanket use of the term [complementarity] is logically empty unless we can say what it would mean for two statements not to be complementary."[14]

MacKay's brief but adequate statement of Bohr's thesis leads him to generalize it differently. It means that "two disparate descriptions can be checked for compatibility only after due allowance has been made for the standpoint from which each is valid."[15] The key concept is thus "difference of standpoint," which MacKay illustrates by appealing to an argument made earlier by C. A. Coulson, namely, that the plan and elevation drawings of a building are complementary to each other in that the views are orthogonal to each other and hence each standpoint is "blind" to the other. He goes on to argue that "each projection exhausts the subject . . . although each leaves undisplayed an aspect of the situation,"[16] a claim which Bedau already has judged to be suspect since no paradox exists between the two projections. So far MacKay has been discussing what he calls "nonhierarchic" complementarity. He holds that there is another kind of complementarity according to which each observer has the same physical evidence available—as, for example, a computer engineer and a mathematician—but their difference in viewpoint lies "in the kind of categories appropriate to each—the kind of cognitive

---

[13]Ibid., 226.   [14]Ibid., 225.

[15]Ibid., 227.   [16]Ibid., 229.

interaction with the subject to which each is made liable by his particular 'state of readiness.' "[17] Thus "the levels of description in such
cases form a hierarchy"; they are each exhaustive and in that sense
complementary.[18]

MacKay insists that there can be no strict analogy between
complementarity in quantum physics and in the science-religion
question because complementarity in microphysics is nonhierarchic
whereas the complementarity of science and religion presupposes
a hierarchic model. Further he argues against Bedau—and I think
correctly—that Bohr's use of the term need not be paradigmatic
since "his aim was to classify and elucidate their puzzling relation
[that is, wave and particle descriptions] by using an already defined
and understood term, not to introduce and define a new term by
pointing to their puzzling relation."[19] Lest we think that MacKay is
advocating "a loose appeal to common usage," we need to be aware
that he does place certain strict conditions on the use of the term
"complementarity," one of which reads "that two (or more) descriptions must, respectively, employ terms whose preconditions of precise definition or use are mutually exclusive."[20] It is apparent that
while necessary it is not a sufficient reason for its use. For the latter
we need to recall the conditions cited earlier: (1) the alteration or
absence of one of the statements would necessitate a change in the
other; and (2) the term "complementary" is "logically empty unless
we can say what it would mean for two statements not to be complementary." After the presentation of a new relational theory of the
complementarity of theology and cosmology it will be appropriate to
inquire whether these conditions have been met or should have
been.

A Relational Theory of the Complementarity
of Theology and Cosmology

The relational metaphysic which will serve as the foundation of
a new theory of the complementarity of theology and cosmology did

---

[17]Ibid., 230.   [18]Ibid.   [19]Ibid., 240.   [20]Ibid.

not come into being for this specific purpose. Rather the thesis of complementarity emerged as a logical conclusion to what was a larger intention, namely, to frame a theory of reality which transcends the classical polarities of subject-object, mind-matter, and so forth. The validity of the case for complementarity rests therefore on the cogency of the relational metaphysic upon which it is based.

It will be impossible, because of space limitations, to present fully the case for a relational metaphysic which I have set forth in another format and which I hope will be available to a larger readership in the near future. What follows is a highly abbreviated version which is presented in the hope that nothing essential to its understanding has been omitted.

The Relational Paradigm

My fundamental thesis is that if one assumes that all relations are internal and from this assumption attempts to derive a coherent theory of reality without assigning priority to mind or world the logical result will be a relational metaphysic in which (1) only relations are regarded as real, and (2) the *relata*—to use classical language—are regarded as derivatives, that is, functional dependencies of relations (to use Ernst Cassirer's language).[21] The initial assumption, that all relations are internal, doubtless will be troublesome to many, as the recent history of debate on the theory of relations confirms. In taking this position I am in agreement with Francis H. Bradley and Brand Blanshard against such philosophers as Bertrand Russell, William James, G. E. Moore, and, most recently, Charles Hartshorne, who have held that either all or some relations are external. In lieu of the detailed presentation and critique of these positions, which I have given elsewhere, I can assert only that a reasonable case can be made for the thesis of universal

---

[21]Ernst Cassirer, "Einstein's Theory of Relativity," in *Substance and Function and Einstein's Theory of Relativity* (New York: Dover Publications, Inc., 1953) 379.

internality, according to which—using the words of Moore—"any term which does in fact have a particular relational property, could not have existed without having that property."[22] My reason for holding this to be true is not complicated. Given aRb, what a is, qua aRb, is defined exhaustively as Rb; what b is, qua aRb, is defined exhaustively as aR. I would venture the opinion that unwillingness to concede this simple principle has been due to the introduction of agenda extraneous to the logically simple case as, for example, when Hartshorne takes aRb as basically asymmetrical for reasons of his fundamental commitment to the notion of temporality. According to his view every relation has a sense or direction, so that one must admit that the earlier (the object) is nonrelative to the later (the subject); the later (the subject) is relative to the earlier (the object).[23] Hartshorne's belief in perceptual nonsimultaneity, which leads him to treat every aRb as having directionality, may appeal to some. My principal objection to it is that it brings a prior understanding to the interpretation of aRb rather than deriving a metaphysic from it.

In an effort to transcend "subject-object" models of perception I have proposed the following "transpolar" law: Given any classical entitative polarities, it is their relation that is real; the polar terms are to be treated as derivatives. The implications of such a law, treated as true, are far reaching. While I cannot explicate these implications in great detail, I do have the responsibility to present the basic tenets of my relational metaphysic since the thesis of complementarity claimed in this essay is grounded on it.

The fundamental claim is that, given any aRb, it is the R(elation) that is real. This position entails the further claim that (1) only relations are real, and (2) all relations are real. As such it represents an inversion of Leibniz's monadology, which held the monads to be

---

[22]G. E. Moore, *Philosophical Studies* (Totowa NJ: Littlefield, Adams & Co., 1968) 288.

[23]Charles Hartshorne, *The Divine Relativity: A Social Conception of God* (New Haven: Yale University Press, 1964) 103.

real and their relations, comprising time and space, to be ideal. I prefer to use the terms "real" and "derivative" rather than "real" and "ideal" to avoid the language of the traditional polarities. My thesis is simply that, given any aRb, a and b are what they are solely by virtue of R.

It follows logically from the fundamental thesis, although the monistic idealists who supported the thesis of universal internality did not draw this conclusion, that all other components of our experience are derivatives of these relations. In what sense are they "derived"? It is reasonable to think that the a's and b's of every aRb—that is to say, the "terms" of the relation—arise from viewing the relation biperspectivally. Thus I use the term "biperspects" as a designation for all terms previously related as classical entities. Derivatives arise as follows: if one focuses attention on ingressive features of any R(elation) as acting, there arises the biperspect a ($=$ acting on); if one focuses on the effective features of any R, there arises biperspect b ($=$ acted upon). They are thus co- or biperspects of the real.

To demonstrate how such a paradigm can account for all the components of our experience, it is necessary to speak briefly about the hierarchy of relations. There is a logical advance from (1) simple relations, that is, aRb considered in its simplest manifestations, which serve as an ontological key; to (2) manifold composites of some relations, whose complexity accounts for the discreteness of the units of experience; to (3) the totality of all relations, which is itself a relation. Reflection on simple relations as a key to the whole of experience led to the logical conclusion that the terms are derived biperspectivally. Since this principle is valid for all relations, it is valid as well for composites of some relations, which are also relations. When viewed biperspectivally, these composites of relations give rise to our common notions of "subjects and objects," "mind and brain," "selves and things," and so forth. These I call "compound biperspects," thus indicating that such notions are coderivative, hence not fundamental. To use Whiteheadian terminology, selves and phenomenal things are abstractions, not concrete entities. To call them actual is to be guilty of the "fallacy of misplaced concreteness." It should be apparent that it becomes inappropriate to opt for Idealism, which makes only the subject concrete, or for Realism, which assigns fundamentality to an objective world. The final hierarchic category, the totality of relations, is explicated on strict analogy with the principle used for simple and composites of relations. If one concedes that the totality of relations is itself a relation—a claim that is fully consistent with the monistic idealists—one will admit the propriety of viewing this totality biperspectivally. If R/totality is viewed ingressively, there emerges the derivative notion of "originative subjectivity," or God-Language. If it is viewed effectively, there emerges the derivative notion of "the totality of the objective world," the physical *universum*, the cosmos. By analogy I call these derivative notions of God-Language and world-language "omniperspects." Theology and cosmology, respectively, represent the modern areas of discourse which deal with these derivative aspects of totality.

It follows from the relational metaphysical schema that neither theology nor cosmology is fundamental, that neither is an ultimate affair. They are coordinate, penultimate insights into reality. "Reality" is the totality of relations which discloses itself to metaphysics.

Complementarity as Relational Biperspectivism

I have tried to show that the thesis of complementarity can be derived deductively from a fundamentally relational metaphysic rather than by being pieced together from apologetic considerations. It is a thesis of complementarity in that it assumes that theology and cosmology are coordinate perspectives on the same domain, that is, the totality of reality. Thus one of the major necessary conditions has been met. Does this theory meet the sufficient conditions laid down by Bedau and MacKay?

The condition established by Bedau is that there must be some legitimate sense of paradox applicable to difficulties relating science and religion. I do not concede that this condition is mandatory since it rests solely on his conviction—to my mind, poorly defended—

that the meaning of the term "complementarity" when used of science and religion is an absolute function of the meaning of the term as used by Bohr. Many physicists and philosophers of science, such as Einstein, Popper, and Mario Bunge, have been unwilling to admit that there is any real paradox even in quantum mechanics, in that they regard only the particles to be "real" in a classical sense. It is tempting to think that the "paradoxes" of the conflict theorists are as "real" as those of quantum physics are to the physicist-philosophers named above. I base nothing fundamental on this observation since I personally hold (1) that there are real paradoxes in quantum mechanics, and (2) that their existence is not essential to the application of the term "complementarity" to other areas.

The two sufficient conditions laid down by MacKay must be taken more seriously. His first, that the alternation or absence of one of the statements would necessitate a change in the other, is somewhat difficult to deal with from my relational perspective since admittedly he is talking about complementary "statements" and I about complementary "systems." If this difference is taken into account, I believe that this condition is met, so long as it is recognized that it would be a complex operation but not an impossible one to determine exactly how a change in one of the systems would require a change in the other.

His second thesis, that the term "complementarity" is logically empty unless one "can say what it would mean for two statements not to be complementary," is simply an analytic judgment following strictly from his assertion that the term is a logical rather than a physical concept. If we try to extend its range to complementary "systems," all that is implied is that something in principle could count against the thesis of complementarity, that is, that it is falsifiable. I am convinced that if one correctly understands the intentionality of both God- and world-language one will concede that in modern theology and cosmology there is emerging a "convergence" toward a relational paradigm as they each independently move toward greater self-clarification. If this is a reasonable claim, there follows from it the expectation that in principle one could say what it would mean for the two systems not to be complementary.

If theology and cosmology are complementary, how does one "complement" the other? To answer this question I must develop at greater length the unique roles of each and attempt to show that each is exhaustive from its standpoint, but penultimate.

In its viable contact with religion, theology is God-Talk. I shall deal exclusively with Judeo-Christian God-Talk since that is our immediate heritage. Theology is concerned with the rational illumination of religious experience. My own theological reflection has led me to develop a relational hermeneutic which judges that the conversion of basically relational insights central to both Judaism and Christianity into a subject-object paradigm of thought inordinately has shifted the center of religious attention away from celebrative participation to epistemological impasses. A symptom of this state of affairs is the recent preoccupation with such issues as theism-atheism, belief-unbelief, and secularity-religiousness, which terminated without resolution in the whole death-of-god madness (*pace* Nietzsche).

This relational metaphysic makes the claim that religious language is to be interpreted exhaustively as an authentic affirmation of the relational nature of experienced reality. It further asserts that Judaism and Christianity reached their heights in participatory affirmations of a divine-human relatedness of ontological significance to both God and man. Another way of saying this is that Hartshorne's insight into the consequent nature of God is faithful to the Western religious tradition. But both Judaism and Christianity were irresistibly tempted by the notion of a nonrelational, remote God, so that preoccupation with God's aseity replaced the original insight of *deus pro nobis*. The Christological formulations, which were—if Torrance is correct—originally fundamental relational statements, were quickly distorted. The earliest insight that Jesus was a paradigm of what is true quickly deteriorated into a nonrelational Christology, thus creating the ontological chasm between Judaism and Christianity. In a relational theology the distinctiveness of both Judaism and

Christianity continues to be affirmed, but it is based on their diverse historical particularity rather than on an ontologically different affirmation.

The complementarity of this understanding of God-Talk with physical cosmology is based on the further claim that theoretical physics is moving rapidly toward relational categories. The replacement of the fundamental particles located in absolute space and time of classical physics with the space-time events of special relativity, the generalizing of classical gravitational theory in the field aspects of general relativity, and the relational implications of observers and events in the Copenhagen version of quantum mechanics—all of these suggest that theoretical physics, to the extent that it is appropriate to say that it reflects the nature of reality, is moving indeed toward a relational model of reality. This claim is likely to be unpopular with those who think of theoretical physics as the study of elementary material particles and their properties. To them I would quote with agreement the insight expressed by Richard Schlegel that physics "does not take any particular set of entities as its subject."[24] Otherwise how can one explain the continuity of physics through the discontinuity represented by the shift in the understanding of entities from classical to modern physics?

Physical cosmology, as a kind of ultimate discipline of theoretical physics, represents the attempt to understand the large-scale structure of the universe, or universes as the case may by. Whatever progress may have been made in this field in this century—and the problems suddenly have become enormous—is a function of the fact that relational models have been introduced into mathematical physics. Cosmologists are learning that nature is a vast, internally related system, and if Sir Fred Hoyle and J. V. Narlikar are correct in their most recent revival of Mach's Principle, the "system" must be regarded as more fundamentally interlocked than previously imagined by physicists.

---

[24]Richard Schlegel, "Quantum Physics and Human Purpose," *Zygon* 8 (1973): 200.

For some, cosmology represents the most sustained successful attempt to understand reality. For others, theology has no equal in this regard. The position of this relational metaphysic is that they are distinct but complementary perspectives on reality. If ultimacy is assigned to either, the result is unproductive. *Theism* in holding God-Talk as fundamental and world-language as derivative is as myopic as *Natural-ism* which takes world-language as fundamental and God-Talk as emotive, attitudinal, or even as obsolete science. The relational metaphysic which has been sketched briefly in this essay arose—autobiographically—from taking both with equal seriousness.

Otherworldliness has been the historical sin of theology made ultimate; indifference and/or hostility to religious language is the unproductive consequence of cosmology made ultimate. It is my claim that both consequences are based on poor perception and self-perception. There is good reason to believe that the deepest insights into both theology and cosmology, from within and without, lead properly to the conclusion that they are coordinate affirmations of the relational nature of reality.

2 | A Relational Reassessment of Myth

A Modern Legacy:
The Rational Assessment of Myth

In the popular mind the term "myth" is frequently set over against "historical," with the result that every story is to be judged "fictional" (= mythical) or "true" (= historical). On this model a historical story as opposed to a mythical one is one that records "what actually happened," to use the idiom of nineteenth-century historians. The judgment that what is mythical is "unhistorical" is the legacy of rationalism. The nineteenth-century claim that the Bible contains mythical material was rooted in the rational critique of religion. The popular notion that mythical means "untrue" was reinforced by the rationalistic attack on the supernatural elements in the biblical tradition. Romanticism, to the contrary, held myth to be the natural medium for religious truth. In Romantic ages myths are born and reborn. As far as the role of religion in culture is concerned, we stand today on the threshold of a new Romanticism.

The current return to a positive appraisal of myth follows an era in which New Testament scholars were preoccupied with what they called "demythologizing." It seemed at first that these scholars were calling for the elimination of myth, that is, for the removal of all unhistorical and unscientific features of the Christian message. Then came the assurance that de-mything the Bible did not mean eliminating the myths, but decoding them in accord with existentialist categories. That there were mythical (that is, unhistorical and unscientific) elements at the heart of the Christian message seemed incontrovertible to a generation obsessed with the spirit of secularity. After all, it seemed self-evident that the New Testament cosmos was simply the prevailing mythical three-storied universe of Late Antiquity, and that the belief in innumerable hostile powers which governed human life from cosmic high places was simply a prevailing religious sentiment. To the demythologizers, such ideas were "prescientific," by which they meant "unscientific" and hence inferior to current scientific views of the universe.

It took a veritable cultural revolution to undo this position and to show that the rational critique of religion, for all its positive gains, had imposed on myth an alien intentionality. It is now more generally assumed that myths do not "intend" to give a description of the world at all, but rather to "image" reality. I should like to add to this view the additional claim that myths intend to image reality as "relatedness." This same intention is manifest even when the myth is narrative in form and so may seem to some to be providing a record of the past, for narrative myths represent but a temporal form put into the service of the imaging of reality as "relatedness."

A Relational Reassessment
of the Jonah Story

It follows from the view expressed above that the Hebrew Scriptures have as their fundamental intention the imaging of reality as relatedness. As a way of illustrating this claim I should like to focus attention on a story from that corpus that continually fascinates its readers, namely, the Jonah story. I venture the judgment that most, if not all, of the traditional hang-ups associated with this story derive from a failure to grasp its intention. The narrative is commonly taken as a pious fiction. Our world is just not like that, it is said. Since the story pivots on fable, some would claim that nothing else in it is worthy of our attention. I should like to argue that the Jonah story is not intended to make us think of a vastly different time epoch in which God, capriciously, played with Nature and mankind. Its intention is rather to image reality as relatedness. In a different idiom, it could be said that the story mirrors the correlation of divine-human reality. We should miss the mark if we should suppose that in this story the divine and the human are separate realities which randomly interact. Rather, God *needs* Jonah to be a revealing God, and Jonah *needs* God to be an authentic human being. I stress the word *needs*; for what I am claiming is that in this story the being of God and the being of Jonah are fundamentally co-realities.

Let me illustrate the meaning of this co-relatedness by appealing to the language of one of modern Judaism's greatest prophets, Martin Buber. Buber represents the heart of biblical religion and human experience by the now-famous term "I-Thou." Even though the book, *I and Thou*, has been around for a long time, we are just beginning to realize that for Buber, the I and the Thou are not two separate, unrelated beings that occasionally enjoy the experience of a relationship. Rather, their being is a co-being. Buber did not mean to emphasize I *and* Thou, but I-Thou. The I and the Thou are co-emergents. This insight was initially suggested to Buber by Feuerbach who had derived the notion rigorously through a phenomenology of human experience.

Have I strayed from the Jonah story? I think not, for the heart of the story is the prayer of Jonah which beautifully illustrates Buber's insight. Since no excerpt from the prayer would forcefully indicate what I mean, I cite the text in full, placing pronouns in italics.

I called to the Lord, out of *my* distress,
and *he* answered *me*;
out of the belly of Sheol *I* cried,
and *thou* didst hear *my* voice.
For *thou* didst cast *me* into the deep,
into the heart of the seas,
and the flood was round about *me*!
all *thy* waves and *thy* billows
passed over *me*.
Then *I* said "*I* am cast out
from *thy* presence;
how shall *I* again look
upon *thy* holy temple?"
The waters closed in over *me*,
the deep was around *me*;
weeds were wrapped around *my* head
at the roots of the mountains.
I went down to the land
whose bars closed upon *me* forever;
yet *thou* didst bring *my* life from the pit
O Lord *my* God.
When *my* soul fainted within *me*,
I remembered the Lord;
and *my* prayer came to *thee*,
into *thy* holy temple.
Those who pay regard to vain idols
forsake their true loyalty;
But *I* with the voice of thanksgiving
will sacrifice to *thee*;
what *I* have vowed *I* will repay.
Deliverance belongs to the Lord!

(Jonah 2:2-9, RSV)

As all prayer, this prayer is in an I-Thou form. The very meaning of prayer is that the I and Thou are really I-Thou. The dialectic of prayer consists in the fact that the monologue is fundamentally a dialogue. Prayer serves as a paradigm to announce that *reality* is *dialogical.*

A Relational Reassessment
of Resurrection as Symbol

A famous logion of Jesus from "Q" preserved in Luke links the Jonah tradition with the Christian affirmation of resurrection. Luke 11:29 quotes Jesus as saying to "the crowds": "This generation seeks a sign; but no sign shall be given to it except the sign of Jonah." We immediately recognize a difficulty with this logion, for it is commonly agreed in the Synoptic tradition that Jesus categorically refused to give signs. The temptation story is the classical instance of this unwillingness. Is this Q logion an exception?

What is a sign that makes its use so problematic from a religious perspective? A *sign* is a convention that points away from itself to what is not present. It tries to overcome the distance between its presence and the absent thing signified. It seeks to authenticate the reality of what is absent. If this definition is accepted, we immediately perceive the inadequacy of signs: they seek to make what is absent seem present. A *symbol,* on the other hand, "manifests as present something that really is present."[1] It is a re-*present*-ation of what is at hand. It is the power of what is present to announce itself.

Can this distinction between sign and symbol resolve the apparent contradiction in the Q logion (namely, "no sign . . . except")? "No sign will be given" would mean "no external authentication of an absent reality to prove its existence." The entire biblical tradition is in harmony with this negative judgment upon miracle for miracle's sake. We should then translate "except the sign of Jonah" as: "except the *symbol* of Jonah." Jonah becomes the symbolic imaging of

---

[1]Hans-Georg Gadamer, *Truth and Method,* A Continuum Book (New York: The Seabury Press, 1975) 136.

reality, here specifically the reality entailed in the notion of resurrection.

With this logion of Jesus we are crossing the threshold into the distinctively Christian tradition, a tradition that has been judged by some, as has the Jonah story, to be mythical, that is, unhistorical and unscientific. What I have developed as a relational model for interpreting the Jonah story I should like to apply exhaustively to the Church's tradition of resurrection faith. The rationalistic judgment that resurrection is a myth implies that it makes historical claims which cannot be justified scientifically. I should prefer rather to argue the case at a different level—namely, that the resurrection traditions, like the Jonah story, have as their intention neither the description of an historical fact of the past nor the verification of a distant God who invades time and space. Rather, the intention of the resurrection traditions out of which the Church arose is the same as that of the Jonah story—namely, to image reality as relatedness. Since it would be difficult to show this directly from the manifold resurrection accounts in the New Testament, I should like to appeal to the later development of the substance of the Christian faith in those centuries in which the Church produced the formal creedal statements of the meaning and reality implied in its faith in Jesus as the Christ.

God-Man:
A Relational Paradigm

It has been common to regard the creedal development in the early Church as the acute Hellenization of the Christian faith, that is, as a deviation from its original intention occasioned by the use of alien Greek philosophical categories to reinterpret the meaning of the Christ. I should like to maintain to the contrary that in the main that development intended to make explicit what was implicit in the Church's faith by giving it a structural form which would protect its central truth in a world vastly different from the historical matrix out of which the faith arose.

It is being increasingly argued that the efforts of the Church Fathers to restate the meaning of Christian belief was not a wildly speculative venture, but one which was characterized by considerable care and restraint. Thomas F. Torrance speaks of the creeds as "disciplined statements"[2] and this can be verified by reading the general theological writings of those Church Fathers who played significant roles in the Church councils. If one looks to the creeds for their most characteristic concept, I think we should agree that it is the phrase, *Very God and Very Man*. The meaning of the Christ is that He is the God-Man. What does that mean and why the choice of a term that is not found *per se* in the New Testament? The answer must be to some extent historical, and to some extent philosophical. Historically: there were those in that day who wished to interpret the Christ in a way which elevated him to Godhood at the expense of his humanity, or limited him exclusively to humanity. Against both views, the Church held to the relational notion: Very God and Very Man. Philosophically: The Fathers were attempting to preserve the relational insight into reality which the God-man paradigm represents. For to elevate Christ to deity or to limit him to humanity would dissolve the relational imaging which this paradigm represents.

What then is the substance of the resurrection faith as given in this paradigm? It is not that Christ is God, nor that he is man; it is not that he is the truth about God, nor that he is the truth about man. It is rather that he, as God-Man, is a paradigm of all reality. In a modern idiom, we should say that he is a paradigm of the co-relational nature of all experience. Christ interpreted as the God-Man is the symbolic re-*present*-ation of the divine and human dimensions of experience. The Jonah story is in this sense fully analogous to the resurrection faith:

> In one idiom we can say: not I *and* Thou, but I-Thou;
> In another idiom: not God *and* Man, but God-Man.

---

[2]Thomas F. Torrance, *Space, Time and Incarnation* (London: Oxford University Press, 1969) 2.

Judaism and Christianity: A Common Intentionality

Why do Judaism and Christianity exist as "two types of faith" (to use Buber's terms) if their myths share a common intentionality? I venture to answer this question by focusing on one essential aspect of the Church's message—namely, the resurrection. While ancient Judaism had little or no use for the concept, probably because of its popularity in the pagan religions of its neighbors, by the time of the ministry of Jesus the concept of resurrection had been sufficiently endorsed by the Jewish communities to influence the Church's faith. However, if we look into the substance of the Christian as opposed to the Jewish notion of resurrection, we become aware immediately that the term, almost from the beginning, was filled with the ideas of death and rebirth; of dying and rising gods; of the rites of Spring; of salvation from hostile cosmic powers of death—all ideas rampant in the pagan world. It should be apparent that the more the Church's faith was informed by the symbols of paganism, the deeper the wedge would be driven between it and Judaism. While I have argued that the Jewish and Christian symbols are alike in imaging the relational nature of reality, it is also clear that the historical forms which their divergent symbols assumed gave them vastly different legacies. Their distinct historical legacies would guarantee that these two faiths would have separate subsequent histories in Western society. What I am insisting is that they do have a common intentionality symbolized in their myths, should they ever wish to pursue the base of their commonality. The faith of the church does not *in itself* alienate the Church from Judaism. Such alienation—at least from the Christian side—is a by-product of a failure to perceive the true intentionality of Christian faith. Christian faith does not have to be defined at the expense of Judaism, as has so often been done.

The Intentionality of Religious Discourse:
The Imaging of Reality as Relatedness

Although much has been said in this essay about intentionality, insufficient attention has been given to its explication. One way of approaching such an explication would be to observe the impact of rational critique on the mythical experience. Viewed from the retrospective position of reason and its critique of myth, the mythical experience is an *undifferentiated* realm. Within that experience certain questions, like those of the existence of the gods, the empirical reality of the mythical cosmology, and the like, simply do not arise; or if they do, they do so on the fringes in a way that serves only to locate the parameters of the mythical experience. When the rational critique of religion arises, however, and it has done so at various times in various cultures, the differentiations that it introduces make the truth-functional questions so fundamental that the question of belief changes even for those within the mythical experience. The result is that the ancient mythical experience is replaced with a more recent version. Not even those who regard themselves as continuing within the religious tradition are able fully to remain within its undifferentiated realm; for reason, too, is a jealous god. One way of restating this point would be to argue that with the rise of religious critique, the intentionality of mythical experience radically changes. Let me illustrate.

Within the closed world of myth the stories serve one primary function, which—as I have said—is to image reality as relatedness. In the Hebrew and Christian Scriptures all the characters, including the deity, are interrelational, as their names suggest. They are all functions of each other, though perhaps not on the same level. The question of the reality of the deity does not arise within the tradition because the denial of the deity would be self-destructive, since they, the self and the deity, are each functions of the other. Nonrelational behavior within the strict rules of this relational intentionality is sin, not unbelief, in the modern sense this term acquired later from rational critique. I would venture the opinion that within the undifferentiated world of myth no one supposed consciously that the proper nouns in the mythical stories are primarily *referential*, that is, that they refer to beings mundane or supramundane, even though within the idiom of the myths the cosmological idiom could later be so construed. The cosmological terms, like "heaven," "hell," and "earth," serve spiritual hierarchical functions rather than spatial ones.

Within its world of discourse religious myth serves to image reality; we should say it is symbolic. Since cosmology is not referential in the myth, but relational, it is speaking of the reality of the only domain of human interest—namely, the sphere of human experience. Myth is imaging the reality of experience. Myth is the disciplined mirror-image of what is fundamental within experience. If one is prepared to trust the interpretations of Buber and myself above on Judaism and Christianity, respectively, what myth points to as fundamental in human experience is *relatedness*.

The term "relatedness" *per se* does not occur within the Judeo-Christian myths. I have chosen it deliberately from the perspective of a relational metaphysics unfortunately too complex to be presented appropriately in this brief essay. Its central thesis can be shared. It is that the most comprehensive, simple, coherent, and fully adequate statement of what is fundamental in human experience is the claim that it is the *relations* rather than the *relata* that are fundmental. Lest this seem unduly esoteric, I should add by way of explanation that the prevailing paradigm of Western thought—which has also served to alter the intentionality of mythical experience—holds just the opposite—namely, that it is the *subjects* and *objects* which are fundamental, while their relationships are accidental and contingent. When this paradigm has invaded the religious sphere of discourse, the characters of the myth are regarded as independent realities which randomly interact. Suddenly the myths become referential *rather* than relational, and the modern questions of atheism and unbelief arise to dominate and so to define modernity.

I am maintaining that the subject-object manner of interpreting experience is not only alien to the mythical experience and when applied to myth alters its intentionality for the interpreter, but is also a poor paradigm for interpreting any experience. It ran into such enormous difficulty in Classical Physics that a revolution was required to preserve the dignity and viability of physics. It is equally problematic in metaphysics in that most of the basic philosophical options between which persons today feel themselves forced to choose are conceptually inadequate because they are based on decisions which make either subjects or objects fundamental. In a relational paradigm no such choice is meaningful, for subjects and objects, rather than being fundamental, are coderivatives from fundamentals (that is, relations). They are not therefore "unreal," but are rather *aspects* of reality. When they are treated as anything more than "aspects," exceedingly complex problems ensue, whether in the interpretation of myth or of nature.

The above explanation about relationality should serve to clarify why the interpretation of myth offered earlier in this essay is so crucial. How many conceptually induced problems in the realm of religious experience can you identify, that is, problems that are not those of religion itself but of its faulty interpretation?

The "modern" theist and atheist alike as they are defined via rationalistic differentiations share the *referential* interpretation of myth: the former affirms that an independent deity exists and the latter that the statement is false. The relational reassessment of myth argues that both claims are the result of forcing an alien intentionality upon myth. The ultimate problem of reason for the mythical experience is not that the former denies what the latter affirms, but that it distorts the meaning of the mythical experience for both. Thus the need for a relational reassessment of myth is vital not only to the *bene esse*, but to the very *esse* of religion itself.

The fundamentality of relatedness announced as Presence through mythical symbols is nondimensional, if by "dimensional" is meant location in space and time. Such dimensionality of reality is an error of interpretation that gives rise to religious exclusivism. The symbolized Presence in Judaism and Christianity does not mean absence in other religious traditions, for the Presentness of Presence is not located in space and time. Presence is the announcement through mythical symbols that reality is relatedness.

3 | Theses
on the Relational Self
and the Genesis
of the Western Ego

From the time I first began to read Fritz Buri's *Theologie der Existenz* and *Dogmatik als Selbstverständnis des christlichen Glaubens* I sensed that his insight into the nature of faith would become a paradigm for my own theological thinking. In the summer of 1963, we first sat together on his terrace overlooking the Rhine and thus began one of the deepest professional associations and warmest relationships of my life. Some time later, when my interest in physical cosmology and philosophy of science developed into a quasi-professional obsession, I found myself looking toward the sciences, and especially physics, for models of reality that might serve as a more exact basis for theological construction. The result of that venture is in some measure shared in this brief essay proudly dedicated to Buri who may fail to see as clearly as I the lines of connection with his programmatic insights which served as the matrix in which I began this independent quest. It seems appropriate on this occasion to begin not with my thought, but with his, as a way of indicating the historical matrix from which I began and the

comparative context for deciding the question of the continuity between his thought and mine.

Of all Buri's deeply insightful works, my favorite is his *Denkender Glaube,* which I assisted in bringing to the attention of the En-
glish-speaking world. Choosing for his title a phrase Jaspers had
coined earlier,[1] Buri approaches the question of *reality* through a
rigorous interrogation of *thinking (Denken).* Out of all the possible
operational questions with which theology can be inaugurated Buri
chooses "What is thinking?" and only out of an answer to that question is he able to identify and "locate" the prime realities of the self
and Being. For Buri all thinking presupposes the subject-object
schema of consciousness (contra Heidegger and Ott), and yet
reaches certain limits, namely, what cannot be thought. At these
limits there is, in Buri's terms, a "Revelation of the Naught," for
there is "disclosed" to thinking a relative and an absolute boundary.
Guided by his existentialist commitments, Buri argues that the subject, the thinking I, can never be objectified. Following his Kantian
commitments, he claims further that Being (= "the totality of
Being," "the totality of the object-world") represents an absolute
boundary, for it is in no sense objectifiable. On the one hand, anthropology which objectifies personhood has limited access to the
real nature of personhood, which Buri feels can only be rendered in
the language of myth, namely, that we stand before the ultimate
mystery that in the infinite expanse of Being a voice resounds sum-
moning us to responsibility in community. On the other hand, cosmology and ontology represent objectifications of what is ultimately
non-objectifiable, and hence do not respect the mystery of non-
being. To speak of Being in view of non-being requires the language
of myth. Being in view of non-being is Grace. With respect to the
limits of thinking consciousness the reality of God is an "impossible
possibility"; but what for thought is mere possibility becomes in
faith reality.

---

[1]"Der Offenbarungsglaube . . . war ein denkender Glaube": K. Jaspers, *Der
philosophische Glaube angesichts der Offenbarung* (1962) 36.

2

In the *theses* below I approach the question of *reality* not through thinking, but through *experience* as this term has been enriched by the American philosophers James and Peirce, and the Japanese thinker Nishida Kitaro. Buri's failure to discuss the wider context of experience per se, of which thinking is but a part, separates his schema from my own. For him, in my opinion, experience is too easily identified with thinking, however much he may protest. Even so, it will come as no surprise to Buri when I shall argue finally that our intentions and the pragmatic sense of our separate systems are similar. By approaching the question of reality through my questions rather than his, however, I hope to effect a formulation that is more open to diverse cultural representations of selfhood and reality. That, however, is something each reader must judge after considering the merits of the theses that now follow.

I. Theses on Pure Experience.
1. The most economical ontological assumption is that experience is all there is. This assumption invalidates metaphysical attempts to locate ultimate reality in a transexperiential domain.
2. The most economical assumption about experience is that fundamental components of experience are accessible only in Pure Experience. All too often, philosophers and theologians have sought the fundamentals solely through an analysis of reflected experience.
3. Pure Experience is characterized by Immediacy.
   a. Immediacy is experiencing; it is Pure Activity.
   b. In Immediacy there is no subject over against an object, hence no Ego.
   c. In Immediacy there is no "prior" or "posterior." There is no "experiencer" prior to "experiencing." There is no "experienced" (thing) posterior to "experiencing."
   d. In Immediacy there are no "intervals": there is no "passing from A to B." Everything is, all at once.

    i. There is no "spatial separation" between Knower and Known.

    ii. There is no "temporal separation" between Intention and Act.

II. Theses on the genesis of the Western Ego derived from the theses on Pure Experience.

  1. The Western Ego emerged partially through attempts to locate the fundamentals of experience by analyzing reflected experience.

  2. Reflection introduces "intervals" which signal the loss of Immediacy.

    a. Methodic, i.e. Cartesian, doubt introduces a "spatial interval" between Knower and Known.

      i. Immediacy is lost because subject and object are separated: the object is "mediated" to the subject. The Ego emerges.

      ii. Methodic doubt is the principal source for the Cognitional Ego., i.e., the thinking subject. This is Descartes's *res cogitans*.

    b. The temporalization of the will creates a "temporal interval" between Intention and Act.

      i. The temporal features of Immediacy suddenly become paradigmatic, with the result that the experience of succession becomes a succession of experiences.[2]

      ii. The temporalized will is the principal source for the Moral Ego, i.e., the introspective subject. The Moral Ego is the "subject" of moral reflection.

III. Theses on a metaphysics of relations.

  1. The most economical assumption about Pure Experience is that its fundamental (i.e., irreducible) components are relations. These are the *res verae*, the only concrete entities. Pure Experience = Immediacy = Activity.

    a. There are no exceptions to the assumption that relations are fundamental.

---

[2]The notion that "an experience of succession is not a succession of experiences" derives from Borden Parker Bowne. My source is P. Bertocci, *The Person God Is,* The Muirhead Library of Philosophy (1970) 52.

   i. All relations are fundamental.
   ii. Only relations are fundamental.
   b. To account for all the features of experience it is necessary to distinguish between simple relations, composites of relations and the Totality of relations.
      i. Simple relations, as the irreducibles of experience, provide the ontological key to reality.
      ii. Composites of (some) relations account for the discreteness of the units of experience and, hence, for "the middle range of the empirical."
      iii. The Totality of relations is a speculative paradigm for the Absolute.
2. It follows that *relata* are abstractions. To ascribe fundamentality (i.e., concreteness) to abstractions is to be guilty of "the fallacy of misplaced concreteness" (Whitehead).
   a. All *relata* must be viewed as derivatives from fundamentals.
   b. Derivatives of relations are co-derivatives: the operation that produces the notion of subject is complementary to the operation that produces the notion of object. Subjects and objects are thus co-derivatives of relations, hence abstractions. This notion of co-derivation is modelled on Laszlo's theory of bi-perspectivism.[3]
      i. The ingressive consideration of a relation produces the notion of subject.
      ii. The effective consideration of a relation produces the notion of object.
   c. Derivatives of simple relations I call simple co-derivatives.
   d. Derivatives of composites of (some) relations I call compound co-derivatives.
      i. The subject-self is to be explained as the ingressive compound co-derivative. This is the origin of the modern notion of the subject.
      ii. Object-selves and object-things are to be explained as effective compound co-derivatives:

---

[3]E. Laszlo, *Introduction to Systems Philosophy. Toward a New Paradigm of Contemporary Thought* (1972) 152.

        (a) The notion of object-self emerges when the relation involves full mutuality;

        (b) The notion of object-thing emerges when the relation involves restricted mutuality.

    e. Derivatives of the Totality of relations I call omni-co-derivatives:

        i. The omni-co-derivative God (= God-Language) emerges from the ingressive consideration of the Totality of relations. This is the basis for speaking of God as person.

        ii. The omni-co-derivative World (= world-language) emerges from the effective co-consideration of the Totality of relations.

        iii. Therefore, theology and cosmology represent complementary (i.e., bi-perspectival) aspects of the same domain.

3. Relations are not "located" in space and time.

    a. Space and time are not fundamentals.

    b. The notions of physical space and time emerge from reflection on Pure Experience.

    c. Physical space and time represent merely the language or logic of measurement.

    d. Pure Activity is always a Now-moment.

4. The "self" of relational metaphysics is the relational self.

    a. The relational self is the self of "Self-Other."

    b. "Self-Other" is an experiential unity.

    c. It is a good approximation to say, with Peter Bertocci, that "the self is what it is doing." In relational metaphysics only an actional definition of selfhood is permitted.

    d. It is not appropriate to speak of a permanently abiding self, since the relational self is not "located" in space and time. The "continuity" of selfhood is therefore not a "passage through time" but a sense of memory.

    e. Memory, the sense of the past, is merely the texture of Immediacy.

    f. For the relational self, the self of Pure Experience, there is only the Now-moment.

IV. Theses on the genesis of the Western Ego derived from the metaphysics of relation.

1. A pseudo-fundamental is a co-derivative that has been accorded fundamentality, i.e., an abstraction that has been treated as concrete.

2. Principal pseudo-fundamentals of Western culture include the subject-self, object-self, objects (e.g., physical things), God, and World.

3. The subject-object paradigm of Western thought that has dominated Western metaphysics by providing it with the alternatives of Idealism and Realism, derives from the erroneous operation of treating *relata* as fundamentals.

4. In the subject-object paradigm of reality relations are treated as contingent, i.e., nonfundamental.

5. The Western Ego is traditionally regarded as "located" in space and time.

6. The Western Ego is an asocial, arelational pseudo-entity which results from according concreteness to an abstraction. Many, if not most, psychic ills are due to this fact of its origin.

V. Theses on the relational Self.

  1. The relational self is the self of Pure Experience.

    a. In Pure Experience there is no differentiation between the self and what it experiences; i.e., in Pure Experience the self is a unity.

      i. Pure Activity is not the product of a "subject." There is only unitive activity from which the notion of "subject" may be derived.

      ii. An "experience" is not the product of an "experiencer"; rather, the "experiencer" is a derivative (i.e., an abstraction) of the "experience" (congruent with Whitehead's notion of "superject").

    b. In Pure Experience "there is not the slightest interval between the demands and the realization of the will."[4]

      i. The "good" is not sought and then found; the "good" must be present from the beginning (Eckhart).

[4]Nishida Kitaro, *A Study of Good*, trans. V. H. Viglielmo (1960) 6.

ii. Time is not a fundamental of Pure Experience. The temporalization of the will which produces the "Moral" (i.e., achieving and failing) Ego is based on an inordinate ascription of fundamentality to time.

2. The relational self is the "I" of "I-Thou."

    a. In the words of Feuerbach who proposed the "I-Thou" paradigm of experience, "The 'I' is merely a linguistic ellipse, that, merely for brevity's sake, leaves out half of what is understood by itself."[5]

    b. In the thought of Buber who enriched the notion by his deeply perceptive insight into reality, the "I-Thou" signals a unifying "Between" (*das Zwischen*).

    c. Feuerbach's and Buber's "I-Thou" is equivalent to the relational self advanced in the relational metaphysics outlined above. The "I" of "I-Thou" is no subject and the "Thou" is no object.

    d. When the unitive "I-Thou" experience is analyzed, i.e., reflected upon, its Immediacy is lost. An "I" emerges, but it is no longer the I of "I-Thou." The I emergent upon reflection is the "I" of "I-It."

    e. The "I-Thou" relation is a function neither of a subject-I nor of an object-self. Rather the subject-I and the object-self are co-derivatives of relations.

    f. The hyphen between "I" and "Thou" does not mark an interval; it is neither conjunctive nor disjunctive. In the "I-Thou" experience there is neither spatial nor temporal separation. In Buber's words, "only the It-World lies in time and space." The "I-Thou" relation is Eternal.

3. The relational self is the self of Christian self-denial.

    a. The most paradigmatic of Christian ideals is self-denial.

        i. The Western Christian teaching of the God-Man reached its apex in kenotic Christology.

---

[5]L. Feuerbach, *Über Spiritualismus und Materialismus besonders in Beziehung auf die Willensfreiheit: Gesammelte Werke*, ed. W. Schuffenhauer, 2. Kleinere Schriften, IV, 1862-1866 (1972) 8.

    ii. The Christian ideal of self-denial is rooted in the self-denial (i.e., kenosis) of the Christ. Self-denial is *imitatio Christi.*

    iii. Christian self-denial is an "emptying" (i.e., kenosis) that is "fulness."

    iv. The emptying that is fulness is the paradox of grace: "Even if a man does humble himself he cannot do it sufficiently, so God has to do it and then the man is exalted. Not that humiliation is one thing and exaltation another, but the highest heights of exaltation lie precisely in the lowest depths of humiliation . . . for depth and height are the same thing" (Eckhart). [6]

b. The most complex of Christian ideals is self-denial.

    i. The temporalization of the will in the West (i.e., the separation of intention from act) created the conditions for the paradox of self-denial.

    ii. Both achievement and failure in moral action intensify the Moral Ego. Both produce introspection.

      (a) The more the Moral Ego strives to achieve self-denial, the farther it moves from its goal.

      (b) Failure in moral action defined as self-denial is, *per definitionem,* an act of the self-bound Moral Ego.

c. The affirmation of the relational character of the self is an affirmation of the ideal of self-denial.

    i. In true self-denial there is not the slightest interval between the intention and the act.

    ii. Where there is no "interval" there is Pure Experience.

    iii. In Pure Experience of moral import there is no "subject" separated from the act.

    iv. Hence, the relational self is not the "subject" of moral acts such as self-denial; rather, the self-denying is the reality.

d. The most adequate approximation to the notion of Christian self-denial in the later history of Christianity is Meister Eckhart's notion of Abgeschiedenheit (= disinterestedness/detachment).

---

[6]R. B. Blakney, ed., *Meister Eckhart. A Modern Translation* (1941) 37.

   i. Genuine "poverty in spirit" is not the result of will.

"As long as a person keeps his own will, and thinks it his will to fulfill the all-loving will of God, he has not the poverty of which we are talking, for this person has a will with which he wants to satisfy the will of God, and that is not right. For if one wants to be truly poor, he must be as free from his creature will as when he had not yet been born. For, by everlasting truth, as long as you will to do God's will, and yearn for eternity and God, you are not really poor; for he is poor who wills nothing, knows nothing, and wants nothing."[7]

   ii. "Poverty in spirit" is not "becoming poor," but "being poor." D. T. Suzuki paraphrases Eckhart's insight with some gain in clarity:

"Our spiritual discipline . . . consists not in getting rid of the self but in realizing the fact that there is no such existence from the first. The realization means being 'poor' in spirit. 'Being poor' does not mean 'becoming poor'; 'being poor' means to be from the very beginning not in possession of anything and not giving away what one has. Nothing to gain, nothing to lose; nothing to give, nothing to take; to be just so, and yet to be rich in inexhaustible possibilities— this is to be 'poor' in its most proper and characteristic sense of the word, this is what all religious experiences tells [*sic*] us. To be absolutely nothing is to be everything."[8]

   iii. Eckhart's admonition to "Get beyond the time!" is fully commensurate with the claim that the relational self is not located in space and time. He wrote, "all time is contained in the present Now-moment."[9]

---

[7]Ibid., 228.

[8]Cited from "Wisdom in Emptiness. A Dialogue by Daisetz T. Suzuki and Thomas Merton," in T. Merton, *Zen and the Birds of Appetite* (1968) 109.

[9]Blakney, *Meister Eckhart*, 212.

4. The relational self is isomorphic with Zen No-Mind.
    a. In Zen Awakening there is no discrimination between subject and object, nor of space or time.
    b. Zen Awakening is neither the result nor the product of a specific state of consciousness. Neither is Awakening a specific state of consciousness.
        i. It is not an object of thought. In states of consciousness subjects are "bound" to objects and hence are not emancipated.
        ii. Nor is it an object of will. There is no Moral Ego.
    c. Zen is the pure act of seeing. According to Hui-Neng, the Father of Chinese Zen, Awakening is chien-hsing, i.e., "to look into the nature [of Mind]." Suzuki summarizes this teaching as follows:
    "The seeing is not reflecting on an object as if the seer had nothing to do with it. The seeing, on the contrary, brings the seer and the object seen together, not in mere identification but the becoming conscious of itself, or rather of its working."[10]
    d. The Zen "act of seeing" is pure, i.e., it is not the act of a subjective state of consciousness, nor does it have as its object "the seen". Suzuki has well stated this doctrine:
    "So long as the seeing is something to see, it is not the real one; only when the seeing is no-seeing—that is, when the seeing is not a specific act of seeing into a definitely circumscribed state of consciousness—is it 'seeing into one's nature.' . . . Paradoxically stated, when the seeing is no-seeing, there is real seeing. . . . As it is 'no-thought' or 'no-mind,' the seeing is really seeing."[11]

---

[10]W. Barrett, ed., *Zen Buddhism. Selected Writings of D. T. Suzuki* (1956) 160.

[11]Ibid., 163.

e. Zen does not accept the dualistic "discrimination" between good and evil that is linked coordinately to Knowledge and the ego. The truth of Emptiness is realized not by "egocentric consciousness" but by the mind; and "when this is done it knows that there is no self, no ego, no Atman that will pollute the mind which is a state of zero. It is out of this zero that all good is performed and all evil is avoided."[12]

f. In Zen there is not the slightest interval between Intention and Act. To illustrate this I shall draw on Eugen Herrigel's reflections on Zen archery:

"For them [i.e. the Zen Masters] the contest consists in the archer aiming at himself—and yet not at himself, in hitting himself—and yet not himself, and thus becoming simultaneously the aimer and the aim, the hitter and the hit."[13]

Having earlier asked his Zen Master, "How can the shot be loosed if 'I' do not do it?," he received the reply: " 'It' shoots."[14] Later he narrates the conclusion to the question:

" 'Do you now understand,' the Master asked me one day after a particularly good show, 'what I mean by "It shoots," "It hits"?' 'I'm afraid I don't understand anything more at all,' I answered, 'even the simplest things have got in a muddle. Is it "I" who draw the bow, or is it the bow that draws me into the state of highest tension? Do "I" hit the goal, or does the goal hit me? Is "It" spiritual when seen by the eyes of the body, and corporeal when seen by the eyes of the spirit—or both or neither? Bow, arrow, goal and ego, all melt into one another, so that I can no longer separate them. And even the need to separate has gone. For as soon as I take the bow and shoot, everything becomes so clear and straightforward and so ridiculously simple. . . .'

'Now at last,' the Master broke in, 'the bowstring has cut right through you.' "[15]

---

[12]Suzuki, cited from Merton, *Zen and the Birds of Appetite*, 107.

[13]Eugen Herrigel, *Zen in the Art of Archery*, with an introduction by D. T. Suzuki, trans. R. F. C. Hull (1971) 6.

[14]Ibid., 58.

[15]Ibid., 69-70.

3

The Basel Münster, where Buri served as Hauptpfarrer from 1957 til 1968, has on its façade a curious equestrian representation of the fourth century bishop, St. Martin. It is curious because alongside the horse stands not a beggar, as is usually the case, but the stump of a tree. In a famous book, *Die Bilder und das Wort am Basler Münster*, Buri cogently argued that this representation originally included the figure for whom St. Martin is dividing his cloak; but that, when the Cathedral was renovated in 1590, the newly proclaimed teaching of the Reformers against "good works" effected an alteration of the original by which the figure of the beggar was "transfigured" into a stump.

In his commentary on the divergent theologies underlying the original and altered versions of St. Martin it is clear that Buri—although committed to the Reformer's doctrine of justification by faith—is not altogether happy about the drastic modification of the original representation on the façade of the Cathedral. For, in his view, the present representation also advocates an extreme position (that is, *ohne Werke*) which has resulted from the success of the Reformation, and which the original, had it been unchanged, could now serve to correct.

The figure of St. Martin on the Cathedral is a symbol of the paradox of Christian *self-denial*. The medieval theology reflected in the original was right in maintaining that the "saintliness" of St. Martin—his true identity—was a function of the beggar with whom he shared his very cloak. Sainthood, in this case, marks the relational self: what St. Martin is, is defined by the "other," the beggar. On the other hand, the Reformers were right in fearing the peril of "egocentricity" latent in this act of sharing, and in judging all moral acts dangerous for this very reason. On this issue it is not difficult to perceive why Meister Eckhart, whose views on self-denial were quoted earlier, is usually claimed to be a forerunner of the Reformation. The moral and religious paradox is that both the original and altered versions of St. Martin are *unsinnig* (to use the term Buri reserves for the latter): the original, in view of Eckhart's deep understanding of *die eigentlichste Armut*; and the altered version, in view of the non-relationality of the solitary figure of St. Martin.

The gift of representing what is not located in space and time is not foreign to religious artists, for their works—like the reality they depict—are always a Now-moment. But their works invite interpretation and herein lies the difficulty. The ontological theme of "relatedness," deeply ingrained in the religious literature and art of our forebears, is all too easily "transfigured" into a "spatiality and temporality" that belies our experience: a "spatiality" in which God "for us" is rendered ultimately inaccessible, and a "temporality" in which the "Good" becomes an Act inaccessible to Intention.

4 | Relational Ontology and Hermeneutics

The current interest in hermeneutics owes much to the impetus it received from Martin Heidegger, who determined, in his *opus classicum, Being and Time*, that subsequent preoccupation with interpretation would be attended by ontological considerations. The question which informs the entire work stands prominently at the beginning: it is *the question of the meaning of Being*.[1] The terms "ontology" and "hermeneutics" in my title betray the influence of Heidedgger upon the effort to find an appropriate modern idiom for rendering the classical theme "Being and Meaning." The term "relational" adumbrates the distinctive thesis to be advanced in this essay.

The theme "Being and Meaning" could in retrospect be said to constitute the haunting philosophical agenda of Western metaphysics. Idealism and Realism, with their respective ontologies of the

---

[1]Martin Heidegger, *Being and Time*, trans. John Macquarrie and Edward Robinson (New York: Harper & Brothers, 1962; 1st German ed., 1927) 19.

subject-and-object-world, represent alternative readings of the relation of being and thought. Idealism is the historic route of those who place thought prior to being; Realism, of those who place being prior to thought. Relational ontology, sympathetic to Hegel's identity of being and thought, conceives being and thought together: being is the presupposition of thought; thought is the articulation of being.

With this introduction the three themes of our presentation have already appeared: ontology, relationality, and hermeneutics. This essay could be construed as an experiment in a new juxtaposing of these fundamental themes.

The dominant role played by epistemology in modern Western thought is largely responsible both for the bifurcation of experience into subjects and objects and for the subjectivist bias permeating Western culture. This bifurcation—deeply ingrained into Western philosophy by Descartes—continues to provide much of the dynamic of our modern world and, as a deep and pervasive paradigm, has governed the conceptual choices of millions as to what they have deemed fundamental and of ultimate worth. The extent to which it has served to limit conceptual options should be apparent from the considerable frustration in our culture, a desperation signaling the presence of a troublesome dilemma. Some of the most notable philosophers of our century distinguished themselves by their measured success in suggesting methodologies or paradigms for resolving this dilemma. Phenomenology represents one of the most sustained philosophical efforts to provide an alternative reading of reality. Heidegger sought to move through phenomenology to primal thinking, to that primordial "thinking of Being" conceived as a subjective genitive. Jaspers's periechontology, his ontology of the Encompassing, represented a strongly idiosyncratic systematization of a unifying—as opposed to a bifurcated—vision of reality. Whitehead, the paradigm for all who seek a comprehensive unification of physics and metaphysics, directed his most sustained critique against bifurcationism. The American philosophers James and Peirce exercised sheer Yankee ingenuity to broaden the base of ontology as historically delivered over to America by German Idealism.

In this essay in the relational ontology offered as an alternative to those subjectivist and objectivist ontologies, certain paradigmatic thinkers have provided significant insights. Leibniz stands for all time as the unique alternative to the pervasive but defective ontology entailed in Newtonian physics. Feuerbach struggled desperately to develop his I-Thou model of reality into an adequate relational option to Hegelianism and materialism; neither the Hegelians nor the materialists could be sure whether he was friend or foe. His last major work, *On Spiritualism and Materialism*, exhibits his finest approach to pure relational categories, but, alas, his approach was asymptotic! It was a pupil of the Viennese editor of Feuerbach's collected writings who would succeed where Feuerbach failed. I refer, of course, to Martin Buber, whose philosophy of the "Between" contains those generic notions essential to a fully relational scheme. These thinkers have been my silent mentors, although somewhat after the fact.

Modern physics has been my chief mentor before the fact. Philosophical insights emerging uniquely in the context of theoretical physics, primarily quantum theory and relativity theory, have been most determinative in the development of the relational theory to be set forth in this essay, although in view of the special focus of this essay I shall not rehearse those details here.

A Relational Ontology

The term "ontology" as used in this essay is intended to denote a theory of fundamentals. Ontology—unpopular since Kant—usually evokes images of the transexperiential, thus provoking the charge that it is entirely a speculative business. Kant spoke of ontology as an abyss from which the rational mind can only recoil in terror. Having suggested in the introduction a possible translation of relational theory into the classical idiom of Western metaphysics, I prefer now to keep closely fixed on the notion of experience as articulated by James, Peirce, Nishida, Whitehead, and, to some extent, Bradley. Thus, ontology as used here will mean "a generalized theory of experience." It seeks to proceed from the simplest assumptions about experience, through maximal generalization, to a comprehensive coherent theory of reality.

If it be objected that all compelling metaphysical schemes have attempted to do the same, a possible response would include the suggestions that other priorities, that is preassumptions, have often intervened to alter the conclusions. Idealistic metaphysics usually proceeds from prior assumptions about the operational priority of epistemology, as I have argued earlier. Realistic metaphysics usually entails prior assumptions derived from uncritical confidence in the *sensus communis*. Process metaphysics, especially as interpreted and defended by Hartshorne and his followers, assumes the fundamentality of asymmetry precisely because of a prior commitment to modal logic, defined by Hartshorne as a "logic of temporality."

Any modern attempt to frame fundamental assumptions can learn much from Kant's choice of questions. The first three of his queries—"What can I Know?" "What should I do?" and "What may I hope?"—betray an already bifurcated world: the "I" over against the "known," the "act," the "anticipated." It is clear that the analytic, reflective process has bifurcated the reality it seeks to understand. The first question splits the unitive experience of knowing into knower-known, that is, it introduces a separation, an interval, into the pure act of knowing, with the inevitable result that the "known" is transfigured into a transcendent object, never really available. The second question introduces a temporal interval between intention and act—a common Western error—and so temporalizes the will. The Good becomes a transcendent object, never fully realizable. The third question splits the unitive act of anticipation into the "I" and the transcendent object, "the future," the result being that the future is never really accessible on Kantian terms, as is evident from his mature work, *Das Ende aller Dinge*. The presence of the "separated I" in Kant's questions betrays the function of prior assumptions which control the possible answers.

The alternative question suggested by Heidegger, "What is a Thing?" avoids the pitfalls of Kant, that is, unless unreconstructed notions of a "thing" endanger its usefulness. A generalized version of Heidegger's question is to be preferred, namely, what is fundamental, and *eo ipso*, what is derivative? *Fundamental* indicates irreducible features of experience, that is, those features which must enter into every fundamental description. *Derivative* indicates proposed fundamentals that ultimately yield to further generalization.

When this operational question is addressed to experience, the most economical answer—and hence the asumption I make—is that *Immediacy* is fundamental. The term "consciousness"—frequently chosen as the synonym for experience—is rejected as too theory-laden. Thanks to the historic essays of James, Nishida, and Bradley, it becomes appropriate to explicate Immediacy in terms of *Pure Experience*. Pure means "prior to reflection," for reflection dichotomizes experience. In reflection the subject is separated from the object. Similarly, methodic doubt splits the unitive act of knowing into knower versus known. Considering the geometrical proclivities of Descartes, it is not going too far afield to label this result a "spatial" separation. Methodic doubt leads inevitably to the assignment of fundamentality to the *res cogitans*. Moral reflection leads to a comparable dichotomizing of unitive moral experiences, so-called acts of will. Such temporalization of the will separates intention from act, thus transcendentalizing the Good. This phenomenon more than any other, perhaps, has determined the special problematic of Western personhood. I should like to suggest that the supposed fundamentals of Western thought—namely, the *Cogito*, the subject-self, the Absolute Ego, the Moral Ego, the object, the object-world—are all conceptual products of reflection. They are not fundamental because they are entities of reflected experience, and reflection destroys Immediacy.

In Pure Experience, known intuitively rather than reflectively, there are neither subjects nor objects. There is only experienc*ing*.

Since there are no subjects, there is no experienc*er* prior to experienc*ing*; neither is experienc*ing* produced by an experienc*er*. There is neither prior nor posterior. There are no intervals, whether spatial intervals between knower and known or temporal intervals between intention and act. It follows from this characterization of Pure Experience that *Immediacy* is *Pure Activity.* Fundamentality inheres in the verbs rather than the nouns, which are usually assigned fundamentality in reflection. The use of the term "verbs" is problematic in view of the subject-object metaphysics built into Western grammar. Given this fact, it might be best to locate fundamentality through the use of the term "infinitives."

The historic connection between subject-object grammar and the theory of relations provides an opportunity to indicate the way in which the appeal to a doctrine of internal relations becomes a defense of reality as Immediacy. Position-taking on the doctrine of relations has determined much of the dynamic of Western philosophizing. With no time here to review the modern debate in detail, I can only announce my commitment to the doctrine that all relations are internal, that is, to the view that *relata* are what they are through the relation. G. E. Moore, an opponent of the thesis of universal internality, has given one of the most precise definitions of the thesis underlying strict internality: "any term which does in fact have a particular relational property, could not have existed without having that property."[2] This means formally that apart from prior metaphysical assumptions, given any relation, that is, any aRb, a is defined by the relation, as is b. This claim is the logical opposite of Russell's theory, which assumed that a and b are "things" entering into relation. And the doctrine of universal internality is a reduction of the views of Moore and Hartshorne, for whom some, though not all, relations are internal. It follows from the simple assumption of internal relationality that *all* relations are fundamental, and *only* relations are fundamental. The *relata* are functions of relating: such

---

[2]G. E. Moore, *Philosophical Studies,* reprint ed. (Totowa NJ: Littlefield, Adams, 1968; first published in 1922) 288.

functions I call derivatives. Because they are coemergent abstractions, I call them *co-derivatives*. It might be asked whether the claims for the nature of Pure Experience and the fundamentality of relations are compatible. My conviction is that they are interchangeable variants entailing the same view of reality. It remains to be shown that this is indeed the case. Pure Experience is an undifferentiated unity; there are no intervals separating subjects from objects. Thus it follows that space and time, quantitatively considered, are not fundamental, for Pure Experience is not located in space and time. Immediacy means a Now-Moment. Space and time can only rightfully be accorded fundamentality to the extent—denied above—that fundamentality can be claimed for subjects and objects. The relational ontology being defended herein asserts, *ex hypothesi*, that relations are not located in space and time. The same claim was made by Leibniz and Whitehead for monads and actual entities, respectively. It is therefore through reflection that the actors (subjects) and the acted upon (objects) emerge. The *ingressive* consideration of a relation results in the notion of "subject," the *effective*, in the notion of "object." These ingressive and effective cooperations abstract from the unitive activity, that is, the relating, and hence yield co-derivatives.

What, it may be asked, are the advantages of this paradigm of relation over the competing options? I shall mention three: (1) it respects the given without disturbing it through reflection, that is, abstraction; (2) it applies one simple principle to the whole of experience; and (3) it does the latter without the reduction necessarily implied in subjectivism and objectivism: neither the subject nor the object is absolutized at the expense of the other, for both are accounted for as coaspectual features derived from experience. Hence, Idealism and Realism are falsified only as isms. The category of coderivative preserves their partial truths while avoiding the debilitating effects that follow when either is made absolute.

I shall now proceed to the presentation of hermeneutical theory rigorously developed from the relational ontology set forth in the first section of this essay.

A Relational Hermeneutics

Hermeneutics is employed in this second section with the meaning "the theory of the meaning of texts, and of specific statements derived from texts." The texts involved are those belonging to the category of "eminent literature," a term made programmatic by Gadamer. Since my primary focus professionally has been on religious texts, I shall develop the theory with special attention to eminent religious texts. The presentation of the relational theory of interpretation will take the form of a theory of the fundamental *intentionality* of myths, that is, of originative religious texts and *eo ipso* of the statements of belief derived from those texts. This theory will necessarily run counter to rationalistic approaches to these texts which, in my judgment, impose upon them an alien intentionality. Over against the demythologizing of religious texts—popular for a generation—I intend to commend a derationalizing of the hermeneutics of originative religious texts.

It is possible to view the whole demythologizing enterprise—to the extent that it was informed by Rationalism—as a struggle not so much with the mythical nature of certain texts as with the modernity of the exegete. The intentionality of myth did not become problematic within mythic experience but from without, namely, from the rationalistic explanation and devaluation of myth. It was precisely the authoritative role of reason in Western culture that generated the kind of critique of myth which—on a relational reading—falls short of understanding. The need for a hermeneutic already signals the loss of mythical-ways-of-being-in-the-world.

The demythologizing debate, which was much broader in scope than Bultmann's historic essay and its aftermath, served to announce the sense of crisis forced upon those within and without religious traditions by the secular ambiance of the last two centuries in the West. At the risk of oversimplifying the issues involved, I propose to thematize what was principally at stake in this debate by affirming the relational intentionality of myth.

The Intentionality of Myth:
Referential or Relational?

In recent generations of scholarship numerous essays have been written on the intentionality of myth. The lack of consensus promotes a further inquiry along relational lines.

To the query "What are myths *about?*" the most common answer would probably be that the myths are "stories *of the gods*." I maintain that within what might be termed prerationalistic mythical consciousness, the questioning ceases at this point except on the defining fringes of mythical cultures. Once that simple naïveté is shattered, the old answer ceases to be adequate both for those who continue within a given religious tradition and for those who define themselves out. Thus, the original question requires reformulation: "What are the stories of the gods *about?*" It was this query, first raised by the Greek Allegorists, that emptied the Olympian Pantheon, for the Allegorists, usually judged uncritical by modern standards, were the first to exercise critical judgment to determine the truth-function of mythical discourse. Prior to that critique the word "myth" meant simply word or story, without the later connotation of fiction.

The insidious effect of the rationalistic demotion of myth is that it not only defines the stance of those no longer sympathetic with the myths but alters the position of those continuing within those respective religious traditions as well. Reason's sovereignty is absolute; for the *differentiae* it introduces alter consciousness so fundamentally that both those within and those without come to assume the same intentionality of myth, namely, that the stories primarily *intend* to *refer* to transcendent beings. Those within the tradition assert that the referential claims are true, while those without assert that they are false, or more cautiously, nonverifiable. The significant fact for us is, not their respective counterclaims, but the implicit agreement that myths are to be understood *referentially*.

The referential theory of myth has no analogue within undifferentiated mythical consciousness, for it is a product of rational judgment. In the relational theory of originative religious stories to be set forth presently, the traditional word "myth" will be used with the single meaning "stories of the gods" and the term "intentionality" will refer to the primary function of such stories within prereflective mythic consciousness. The relational theory of myth entails the negation of the referential theory, based on the judgment that the latter is grounded in a subject-object paradigm of reality. Such a judgment assumes that a different ontology will issue in a hermeneutics of myth consonant with its assumptions about reality. Fundamental to the relational ontology already presented is the attendant hermeneutical principle that myth is to be interpreted *relationally.*

The Intentionality of Myth
as the Imaging of Reality as Relatedness

This claim will to some appear a bold assertion, partly because to them it may seem to run counter to conventional notions of both myth and reality, and partly because it may seem that a reduction of the intention of myth is thereby effected. In order to justify the relational claim under consideration, I shall return to the simple definition of myths as "stories of the gods." The component "of the gods" indicates what the stories are about *within* what Ricoeur calls the first naïveté. Although the narratives portray actions of divine beings, the originative religious stories give no attention to their reality *per se.* That is not an oversight. The myth is a closed world; no one steps out of it to supplement the narrative. This fact leads us to consider the literary phenomenality of myths, namely, that they are *stories.* As such, understanding what they *tell* is understanding all they *intend.* A story is both *disclosure* and *limit.* What it intends, it conveys; what it does not convey, it does not intend. The task of the interpreter is solely to understand what it intends and to respect what it does not intend. I argued earlier that the referential theory of myth overlaid on myth an alien intentionality. Now

I can add by way of clarification that the theory failed to respect the limits of the story. Note carefully what is being claimed in my indictment: it is not that the story *announces* limits but rather that the story as story *is* limit. There is no legitimate transgressing of these limits, whether in the interest of establishing the transcendent reality of the deities named in the stories or for the purpose of reconstructing some presupposed past of which the myths are thought to be a record. If these are illegitimate pursuits, what—it may be asked—are legitimate claims for the intentionality of myths that respect their narrative limits?

I suggest, along strict relational lines, that myths image reality as relatedness. I maintain, further, that the most economical reading of the stories, and hence the one most commensurate with their intentionality, notices one thing: characters in relation. The characters cannot be lifted out of the relationships, for in a fundamental sense they *are* the relationships. The primary disclosures given in the reading are neither clues to the existence of these characters in relation (the *dramatis personae*) "outside the story" as it were, nor guides to the reconstruction of what actually happened in the past life, that is, in the supposed real time of the characters. All such expectations derive from the referential paradigm. The religious stories commend themselves, rather, for their aesthetic and paradigmatic imaging of reality as relatedness. In light of what was claimed earlier about ontology and experience, it is appropriate to extend the statements about the intentionality of myth a step further: myths are archetypal images of what is fundamental, namely, *Pure Experience, Immediacy, relating*. The myths archetypicaly image the same insight into reality that emerges in relational ontology. Nevertheless myths are not ontologies. The terms "archetypal" and "image(ing)" express the difference. It is the second of these terms I should like to develop first. Clarification of the first will appear later.

Imaging is what myths do. That they do it successfully is largely an aesthetic affair. One could say that the imaging they do is aesthetic disclosure.

I am not suggesting that this latter term "disclosure" entails the ancient doctrine which interprets the phrase "of the gods" as a subjective genitive. Disclosure is used here in one sense only: in myth what is present is re-*présent*-ed. Following Gadamer, I interpret myth as the re-*présent*-ation of what is at hand.[3] The proper synonym for myth is thus symbol. One way of amplifying the meaning of symbol is to differentiate it from a sign, the latter being an arbitrary convention that points away from itself to what is not present. A sign thus *sign*-als the reality of what is absent. Its inadequacy lies in the distance between its presence and the absent thing signified. It seeks to authenticate the reality of what is not at hand. Hence the great reticence of archetypal religious persons to provide signs, as for example, when Jesus in the synoptic accounts announces, "No sign will be given you except the sign of Jonah" (Matt. 12:39; 16:4; Luke 11:29). I would resolve the apparent contradiction in this saying ("no sign except") by arguing that the first occurrence of the phrase "no sign" carries the meaning assigned to the term in my previous discussion, while the meaning of the final phrase is best captured in the translation "instead I give you the symbol of Jonah." Mark's simpler form, "no sign will be given this generation" (8:12), becomes commensurate with Matthew's and Luke's versions with the suggested interpretation of the latter. It also follows that the proper rendering of the key word σημεῖον in the Fourth Gospel is symbol rather than sign.

In contrast to signs, symbols re-*présent* the power of what is present to announce itself. Put more forcefully, *Presence* is the announcement of reality as relatedness. Thus for relational hermeneutics the intentionality of myth is in full accord with the relational ontology outlined above.

I shall now indicate some of the implications of this relational understanding of myth and, in the process of doing so, shall take the

---

[3]Hans-Georg Gadamer, *Truth and Method* (New York: The Seabury Press, 1975; 1st German ed., 1960; 2nd., 1965) 136. Gadamer's wording is "a symbol manifests as present something that really is present."

occasion to amplify some key notions only hinted at so far. Attention will be confined to two implications that seem to be the most far-reaching for the interpretation of religious texts and of statements of belief modeled on them, namely, (1) the negation of the view that originative religious texts are historical records, and (2) a reinterpretation of the transcendent dimension in the stories that defines them as religious.

The Rise and Fall
of the Faith-History Paradigm

The real shibboleth of recent generations of Scripture scholarship in the West is neither the term "kerygma" nor "hermeneutics," as is commonly supposed, but the term "history" and its cognates "historical" and "historicity." Those conversant with the ebb and flow of the various modern schools of interpretation of Scriptures that have successfully commanded the loyalties of Jewish and Christian scholars will realize how pervasive the term "history" has been in defining their principal differences. As one long caught up in this phenomenon, I now wonder why it exercised control over my mind for so long; and, further, why modern sacred phrases like "God acting in history" and "the historical Jesus" seem to lose their cogency, and hence their urgency, once a relational theory of religious texts is espoused.

The claim that a deep commitment to historicism permeates modern Western scriptural interpretation needs no documentation. The unexamined assumption of that historicism is that *narrative* implies *record*. Anyone conversant with the complex character of modern biblical criticism over the past two centures is aware of the extensive investment of energy directed toward the reconstruction of "what really happened" behind the documents, whether it be the lives of the Patriarchs, the deeds of Moses, or the life of Jesus. I am well aware that in recent scholarship objections have been raised about these efforts at reconstruction on the grounds that faith is not well served by such activities. I should like to suggest a more text-related objection, namely, that these well-intentioned exercises in historical reconstruction do not respect the *limits* of the stories as stories. To treat such narratives as records, whether judged historically valuable or worthless, results in a shift away from the stories to what is not present, that is, to some previous time in which the actions are thought to be located. In such treatment the text ceases to function as *image* or *symbol* and becomes an *organon* for solving questions foreign to originative religious texts. The result is that the text—as we used to say—becomes a pretext.

My remarks are not to be construed as a negative judgment on the work done legitimately by historians. Such interests seem essential to the self-consciousness of a civilized culture. What we learn from historians of genius, moreover, is that texts are also historical phenomena, often of significance equal to, or greater than, the events supposedly reported in texts under consideration by the historian. It must also be noted that certain newer methodologies in Scripture scholarship—as redaction criticism, literary criticism, structuralism, genre criticism, and such—seem to be more aware of the need to respect the narrative-text as *limit*, that is, as something in itself.

The legitimate extension of the principles of this relational hermeneutic to all texts of "eminent literature" should be apparent, especially to those who have pondered the deeply perceptive hermeneutical insights of Gadamer, expressed programmatically in his work *Truth and Method.* That I came to so similar an understanding of hermeneutics out of a quite different matrix reinforces my confidence in the viability of this relational theory of interpretation. Whether the relational ontology from which it is derived would be attractive to him I cannot say. I should now like to develop the theme of the religious dimension of myth.

The Religious-Transcendent Dimension of Myth

Lest it seem that relational hermeneutics is insensitive to the religious dimensions of myths, I shall attempt to explicate in relational terms what the expression "of the gods" means within mythic consciousness. What follows is intended to apply with equal validity to originative religious stories and to statements of belief modeled on them.

The first step toward this explication is the simple translation of the phrase "stories of the gods" into the generic formulation *God-Language*. Some might prefer the term "God-Talk," suggested by Macquarrie, but they must bear in mind that he coined it as a characterization of theology. God-Language seems to me best suited to represent the distinctive dimension of mythical discourse.

God-Language, suggested by the primordial symbols of mythical stories, functions, as does every symbol, both as *disclosure* and as *limit*. As was claimed earlier, myths disclose through imaging. The question as to what is disclosed has partially been answered by the attendant claim that myths image reality as relatedness. To the extent that this claim is interpreted exhaustively as the nature of experience, no transexperiential conclusions being admitted, this interpretation of God-Language appears formally similar to Bultmann's theory that the task of the interpreter is to explicate the understanding of existence the myth is trying to express.[4] The existentialist anthropology Bultmann developed as the exhaustive disclosure of myth functioned well for a generation suspicious of ontology. A rationalist corollary of this existentialist reduction was the call to eliminate the cosmology in which the story was set. A relational reassessment of myth does not proceed by eliminating anything; rather, it treats the myth as an inviolate whole. As I see it in retrospect, Bultmann made two questionable assumptions fatal to his program, the first being that *pre*scientific means *un*scientific, hence untrue,[5] from which it follows that the cosmological elements

---

[4]Rudolf Bultmann, "The New Testament and Mythology," in *Kerygma and Myth* I. ed. Hans Werner Bartsch (London: S.P.C.K., 1953; 1st German ed., 1941) 16.

[5]The problematic character of Bultmann's assumptions about modern science was pointed out early on by Karl Jaspers, in "Myth and Religion"; cf. *Kerygma and Myth* II, ed. Hans Werner Bartsch (London: S.P.C.K., 1962; 1st German ed., 1948) 133ff.; 143-44.

must be stripped away if one is to understand myth. This dubious assumption originated within his rationalistic bias against primitive modes of expression. The second assumption was that myth "speaks of the other world in terms of this world, and of the gods in terms derived from human life."[6] The relational hermeneutics advanced here argues the inverse, namely, that in myth this world is presented in terms of the other world, that is to say, experience in terms of God-Language. The net effect of this inversion is to focus the interpretation of myth on experience; the transexperiential is excluded *per definitionem*. That this move entails no reduction of the essential function of God-Language—whether as present in originative religious stories or in statements of belief modeled thereon—remains to be shown.

The explication of the character and function of God-Language forces us back to the ontological priority of relation. While it has been maintained in this essay that objects and object-selves are—like subjects—derivative notions, I have carefully refrained from referring to these objects as forms of experiential otherness. For it is central to the relational paradigm that in Pure Activity the experiential self and experiential other are not yet differentiated. Unlike coaspectual derivatives, their reality is coactuality, mutuality. A vestige of this relational affirmation lingers in the coaspectuality of the subject-object derivatives. Only the notion of mutuality functions ontologicaly in the delineation of the complex character of otherness which follows:

(1) when the experiencing entails *restricted* mutuality, the experiential other yields upon reflection the notion of phenomenal things:

(2)When the experiencing entails *full* mutuality, the experiential other yields upon reflection the notion of object-selves.

Myth represents the fundamentality of mutuality dramatically and eminently through a characterization distinguished by the primary role of the Eminent Other. Failure to understand the narrative

---

[6]Bultmann, "The New Testament and Mythology," 10.

character of myth has led to the interpretation of the Eminent One as "the Wholly Other," a notion which appears erroneous in view of the intrinsic mutuality of otherness. The fact that myth as been so interpreted is best explained by the *allzumenschlich* proclivity for ontologizing derivative notions, a state of affairs bemoaned by Whitehead in his classic phrase "the fallacy of misplaced concreteness." Only through a referential reading of God-Language does myth express Absolute Otherness. Relationally interpreted, God-Language is the announcement of the Eminent Other. Does such a claim entail the legitimacy of interpreting the Eminent Other as person? It would seem that the ascribing of personhood to God is tantamount to the ascribing of independent subjectivity to object-selves, raised to the eminent degree. There is some support for this suggestion from a statement in Whitehead's *Process and Reality*:

> Creativity is here termed "God", because the contemplation of our natures, as enjoying real feelings derived from the timeless sources of all order, acquires that "subjective form" of refreshment and companionship at which religions aim. [7]

The unique feature of God-Language, usually expressed by the term "transcendence," I have called *eminence*. Eminence means that God-Language represents a derivative imaging of experience-considered-as-a-Totality, coaspectual with "world-language," or cosmology. Such is the basis of my view that theology and cosmology are complementary, that neither is absolute. [8]

The eminence of the Other lies, not in some presumed "primordial nature" of the Other, but in the eminence of certain relations, expressed in words like worshiping, reverencing, trusting, believing. An example may add a dimension of clarity to the highly

---

[7] Alfred North Whitehead, *Process and Reality: An Essay in Cosmology* (1929; Harper Torchbooks reprint edition (New York: Harper and Row, 1960; first published in 1929) 47.

[8] Cf. essay 1 in this collection.

idiosyncratic language I am using. Take two sentences, grammatically similar:

A. I trust (a) person.

B. I trust (in) God.

In sentence A, relationally understood, the "I" and the "person" are regarded as derivatives of the fundamental activity, "trusting." It is the dimension of full mutuality inherent in the verbal notion of "trusting" that yields the coderivative, "the personal other." That same mutuality inheres by analogy in the verb "trusting" in sentence B, though every user would admit that it is raised to the eminent degree. Since no ontological principle deriving from the relational ontology presented in this essay warrants the category of "eminent mutuality," it is apparent that in sentence B, we have to do, not with God-as-*the*-Other, but with the Eminent Other, that is, with God-Language. We are, in sum, dealing with myth, whether in the form of "eminent literature" or of belief statements utilizing its prime categories. This conclusion supports the definition of myth throughout this essay as *stories* of the *gods*. In myth, interpreted rigorously in terms of a relational paradigm, one has to do, not with God existing *beyond* (that is, *trans-*) experience, but rather with the other of eminent imaging, that is, with a coaspectual imaging of experience-considered-as-a-Totality.

The reference to religious acts invites amplification. Such acts are not categorically distinguished by the usual criteria of (1) greater intensity, (2) ritual or moral purity, or (3) the eminence of the object. Rather, they merit the qualifier "religious" because they (re)-en-act the myth. Through religious acts the religious person dwells within the mythical matrix of meaning. No one worships save within the matrix of myth: thus worshiping is an entering into mythic drama in the role defined for devotees by the myth. For this reason myth and ritual belong to the very essence of religion.

5 | Western Introspection and the Temporalization of the Will

As it is meaningful to speak of Western culture, so it is meaningful to speak of "Western personhood," signifying thereby instances of individual and social orientation informed primarily by the historic cultures of Europe and the eastern Mediterranean. The rapid advance of planetization—to use Teilhard's neologism—has occasioned an increasing awareness of precise differences between East and West, and consequently of those characteristics that are distinctive of Western personhood. Broadly conceived, the intention of this essay is to take a selective look at Western personhood and thereby to explore the extent to which *who* and *what* we are is a function of our distinctive heritage and the interpretation we have chosen to place upon it.

Modern Western personhood represents a complex tapestry of cultural threads so intricately interwoven that the tracing of individual features to distinct origins is virtually impossible. Each individual in the West represents a unique tableau, a detailed configuration within a larger cultural composite that determines in large measure the framework of individual life. That large composite comprises Western culture with its special languages, values, concepts, prejudices, habits, taboos, beliefs, and more.

The assumption behind this essay which focuses on the distinctive contribution of Western Christianity to the shaping of modern Western personhood, is that such a contribution has been truly all-pervasive—truly ecumenical—in a way Christian doctrine *per se* has never been. To achieve this goal some reinterpretation of Western Christianity will be proposed. I should also add that, while the theory of relational selfhood to be presented in this essay grew out of a larger metaphysical work several years in the making,[1] the specific thrust of this essay owes much to the inspiration and insights of Krister Stendahl.[2] While I have some reason to believe he might be sympathetic with some of the conclusions of this present essay, I must nevertheless take full responsibility for the use to which I put his ideas.

Stendahl's phrase, "the introspective conscience of the West,"[3] strikes me as especially apt for describing what I call the "subject-object" orientation of modern Western culture with its proclivity for subjectivism. When I thought to isolate the part played by Western religiosity in the emergence of this so-called subject-object "paradigm," Stendahl's deeply perceptive rethinking of the course of Western theology seemed ready-made for my task. My readiness to adopt his term "introspective conscience" rested on the fact that it signalled a quality in Western selfhood I had isolated through other means. Prior to reading Stendahl's provocative essays, my own commitment to the notion of Paul's "plagued conscience" hindered my own rethinking of the relationship of historical theology to its biblical foundations.

---

[1]Harold H. Oliver, *A Relational Metaphysic* (The Hague: Martinus Nijhoff Publishers, 1981).

[2]Krister Stendahl, *Paul among Jews and Gentiles and Other Essays* (Philadelphia: Fortress Press, 1976).

[3]Ibid., 78-96: "Paul and the Introspective Conscience of the West."

Students of Augustine's *Confessions*—one of the first deeply significant psychological texts in Western civilization—are aware of the extent to which the term "plagued conscience" suits the temperament of that great work, especially as depicted in the opening chapters. However one may feel about the traditional thesis that the theological roots of this phenomenon of the "troubled psyche" lay in Romans 7 and in the Pauline literature in general, there is no denying that with Augustine a paradigm of subjectivity is established with such forcefulness as to condition Western piety for centuries to come. With a deep debt to Tertullian's legalizing of Christian idiom, Augustine's sense of the "plagued conscience" dominated medieval piety, a late form of which constituted the matrix of Luther's theology, and—if Stendahl is correct—also provided the hermeneutical key to Luther's interpretation of Paul.[4] Stendahl has performed a vital service to biblical theology by cogently arguing that Augustine and Luther, both unaware of the original context and import of Paul's doctrine of justification, "modernized" the Apostle's thought by the norms of their own religio-cultural problematic. Of special importance for the present essay is Stendahl's faithful tracking of the emergence and entrenchment of the Western "introspective conscience" through a process that determined that Roman Catholic and Protestant notions of personhood would vitally link these traditions in a more fundamental way than their rival doctrinal pronouncements should lead us to expect. Historic Protestantism monumentalized the sense of personhood prevalent in late medieval piety through the mediation of a doctrine of justification "applied in a consistent and grand style to a more general and timeless human problem"[5] rather than to the specific issue of the relation of Jews and Gentiles which Stendahl claims was Paul's central concern.

Permit me two historical notes before turning to a thematic consideration of the grounds for the emergence of the Western intro-

---

[4]Ibid., 85.

[5]Ibid.

spective conscience. (1) Eastern Orthodox Christianity, truly neither Eastern nor Western in the general cultural sense of these terms, remained principally unaffected by the Roman tradition of the troubled psyche, being for this reason a historic testimony to the adventitious character of the link between Christian theology and the Western psyche, as well as a viable alternative to the "wretched" self-image of Western personhood inherited along a different route. Anyone familiar with the principal ideas of Gregory Palamas or the Cappadocians will have firsthand knowledge of a different "feel" of experience than that prevailing in the West. (2) It is important to recall that at least one key figure in the West, Meister Eckhart, not only rejected the Augustinian sense of time and personhood, but actively preached against it in terms of a doctrine of self-denial which I find to be fully commensurate with the biblical roots of personhood.[6]

The Unity of Experience
and Its Western Bifurcation

It has long been recognized, and most recently emphasized by Heidegger, that Cartesian doubt signalled the emergence of the notion of the modern subject, a fateful event for Catholic and Protestant theology alike. The impact of Descartes's bifurcation of selfhood into the *res cogitans* and the *res extensa* was mediated to modern theology through the transformation it received at the hands of Kant, especially in his first *Critique*. I have come to be convinced of Heidegger's thesis that the first *Critique* assumed the priority of the Cartesian subject to such a degree that the singular problem it addressed was "the objectivity of the object."[7] If we focus

---

[6]Cf. essay 3, above.

[7]Martin Heidegger, *What is a Thing?*, trans. W. B. Barton, Jr. and Vera Deutsch, with an analysis by Eugene Gendlin, Gateway edition (Chicago: Henry Regnery Co., 1967) 55.

momentarily upon Kant's three historic questions, "What can I know?", "What must I do?", and "What may I hope?", we are struck by the fact that his approach to these fundamental human experiences prejudged the kinds of answers that are to be expected—indeed that are even possible. The first question, "What can I know?", prejudges "knowing" on two counts: (1) it treats specific "knowing" as a question rather than a reality; and (2) it assumes the separation of the subject of the act (that is, the "knower") from the object (the "known," or better, what is to be known). Objects of knowing are thereby transcendentalized, that is, made ultimately inaccessible, by the way the experience of knowing is addressed. Kant was forced by his separation of "knower" from "known" to the treatment of the experience of knowing as a question. The second question, "What must I do?", prejudges moral acts on the same two counts. "Good" is transcendentalized into "the Good," that is, into what is finally inaccessible *an sich*. For my purposes it is important to argue that Kant introduced a spatial interval between "knower" and "known," and a temporal interval between the moral "subject" and its act (between Intention and Act). The term "spatial" is justified in view of Descartes's proclivity for geometry, and the term "temporal," in view of the special nature of moral action.

We are so accustomed to reading experience through Kant's eyes that it seldom occurs to us to think of it differently. What would emerge should we assume from the outset the unity of experience, both cognitive and moral? In the article mentioned earlier I set forth a theory of the unity of experience commensurate with William James's and Nishida Kitaro's notion of Pure Experience.[8] In view of the needed independence of this present essay I may be permitted to restate the essentials of that theory of the relational self.

Pure Experience, that is, what precedes reflection, is a unitive act. Subject is not yet differentiated from object. There is neither "prior" nor "posterior." The subject does not "produce" the action, for there is no experienc*er* prior to experienc*ing*. There is no ex-

---

[8]Cf. fn. 5, above.

perienc*ed* thing or person posterior to experienc*er* or experienc*ing*. It follows that Pure Experience is a unity, undifferentiated with respect to these so-called "parts" or "modes." As an undifferentiated unity Pure Experience is Immediacy, Pure Activity. What *is*, in a fundamental sense, is experienc*ing*, act*ing*. Therefore I make the claim that experience (experiencing) is all there is. It further follows that experiencing is "relating," that is, that it consists exhaustively of *relations*. The *relata*, such as subjects and objects, mind and brain, and so forth, can only be accorded the status of derivatives, that is, abstract notions.

It is through reflection that unitive experiencing yields analytic parts such as "subject" and "object," "prior" and "posterior," for reflective analysis is by its nature a focusing upon what is no longer immediate. From the standpoint of relational ontology these notions cannot be accorded fundamentality. The Western custom of assigning fundamentality to them accounts for the emergence and longevity of the historical options of Idealism and Realism.

A further word about "prior" and "posterior." These notions as well as those of "here" and "there," designate derivative features of experience. Physical time and space are derived from features of experience, but—as they function in modern physics—represent no more than the language of measurement. In modern physics, informed by quantum and relativity theory, "things" are no longer said to be "located" in space and time. Even the usual notion of "thing" has been replaced by that of space-time events. Nevertheless there remain philosophers and theologians who continue to use this questionable idiom in the fundamental way in which these notions functioned in Newtonian Physics. The result is often "a misplaced concreteness" applied to time and space. As I have tried to indicate, this practice renders cognitive and moral activity problematical. Of greatest consequence in the West is the support it gives to the phenomenon of the "plagued conscience" and its spiritual cognate, the Moral Ego.

The Temporalization of the Will
as the Transcendentalizing of "Good"

The bifurcation of moral action in the West has produced the illusion (among Westerners!) that Western religiosity is more committed to moral concerns than is the case with Eastern religions. John Cobb recently defended the thesis that while Buddhism and Judeo-Christianity have shared the quest for the metaphysical ultimate, the latter—Judeo-Christianity—is fundamentally to be distinguished from the former by the quest for a second ultimate (*sic*), namely, the principle of rightness.[9] While I am not ready to challenge the second part of his thesis *en toto*, I am basically uncomfortable with the idea of a second ultimate. The principle of rightness probably did function as the determinative factor of *Western* Christianity, but the different sense of moral experience in Eastern Orthodoxy should serve as a *caveat* to those who would regard it as an essential component within Judeo-Christianity prior to the late second century. There is a tendency among Roman Catholics and Protestants to project their own perceptions of rightness back upon their ancient traditions, as for example, when Luther projected the problematic of late medieval piety upon the Pauline world of Romans 7. If this practice entails an erroneous assumption, there is good reason to initiate a fresh examination of the moral dimension in the Jewish and Christian biblical traditions.

The separation of Intention from Act, that is, the temporalization of the will, may well be the *fons et origo* of the phenomenon of the "plagued conscience" so characteristic of medieval and modern Western Christianity. That this is a "temporal" separation should come as no surprise, for it originated within that region of Christendom in which the qualitative temporality of biblical eschatology

---

[9]John Cobb, "Buddhist Emptiness and the Christian God," *Journal of the American Academy of Religion* 45 (1977): 11-25.

was transfigured into a quantitative, that is, linear, historical time. It is surely of fundamental significance that it was Western Christianity that welcomed the Apocalypse of John with open arms and treated it as the principal repository of iconographic imagery, whereas in Eastern Orthodoxy the Apocalypse was still unwelcomed as late as the tenth century. Such basic observations go a long way toward explaining the rise of historical consciousness and historiography in the West, a phenomenon which Eastern Orthodoxy still views with some suspicion.

The difficulties which Meister Eckhart encountered in his predominantly Augustinian culture remind one both of the monolithic character of that culture and the utter strangeness of his vision of moral and religious experience to most of his contemporaries. I am convinced that his insights are more faithful to the roots of our religious heritage than those of the Augustinian legacy which still defines modern Western Christian self-perception. His fundamental commitment to the ancient teaching on self-denial threw the whole of late medieval piety into confusion; and while Protestant theologians claim him as a forerunner of their Reformation, my sense is that his deep grasp of Christian selfhood constitutes as much a judgment on Protestant piety as on the piety it sought to replace.

The notion of self-denial is a uniquely fruitful category for reaccessing what is fundamental to Christian experience, despite the fact that Western Christianity has never known what to do with that component of its legacy. After all, how can one take it seriously in view of the fact that self-denial seems to be a *contradictio in adjecto*, in that it is grossly self-serving to strive for it, and a sign of egocentrism not to undertake it.

What one learns principally from a study of Eckhart's reformulation of the Christian notion of self-denial is that a false claim for the fundamentality of time lies at the root of the paradox. His most significant insight is captured in the title assigned to one of his sermons by a modern editor: "Get beyond time!"[10] Before we are tempted to

---

[10]Raymond Blakney, ed., *Meister Eckhart. A Modern Translation,* Harper Torchbooks edition (New York: Harper & Row, 1941) 212-17.

write this off as mystical escapism, we should do well to review his teaching on self-denial and the fundamental reconceptualization of temporality it entails. Nothing was more central to medieval life than the notion of poverty and its concomitant, almsgiving; for the latter—"giving away all one has"—is supposed to produce the former. But since it is what one *has* that one gives away, one is faced with the temptation to take pride in the achievement. The result is that the state of poverty produced is not really "poverty," in that the Moral Ego which emerges represents a selfish "fullness" rather than a real emptiness. Eckhart saw only one way out of this dilemma: genuine poverty cannot be an act of the will. His words are instructive:

> As long as you will to do God's will, and yearn for eternity and God, you are not really poor; for he is poor who wills nothing, knows nothing, and wants nothing.[11]

Deeply conscious of the link between Eckhart's notion of self-denial and his sense of time, D. T. Suzuki locates the Western moral dilemma in its all too easy translation of self-denial into *"becoming poor."* In place of this temporalizing of moral action, Eckhart held to the more fundamental notion: *"being poor."* Suzuki's paraphrase of Eckhart's insight faithfully and succinctly gives the sense:

> "Being poor" does not mean "becoming poor"; "being poor" means to be *from the beginning* [my emphasis] not in possession of anything and not giving away what one has. Nothing to gain, nothing to lose; nothing to give, nothing to take; to be just so, and yet rich in inexhaustible possibilities. . . . To be absolutely nothing is to be everything.[12]

Those trained in the Augustinian legacy will interpret the phrase "from the beginning" in a linear temporal sense and will therefore

---

[11]Ibid., 228.

[12]"Wisdom in Emptiness. A Dialogue by Daisetz T. Suzuki and Thomas Merton," in Thomas Merton, *Zen and the Birds of Appetite* (New York: New Directions, 1968) 109.

judge this reformulation of self-denial to be as paradoxical as the paradox it sought to unravel. To grasp the utterly different sense the phrase had for Eckhart one has only to meditate deeply on the sermon, "Get beyond time!" The foundation of his argument is that "all time is contained in the present Now-moment," that is, God's day.[13] The "soul's day," on the contrary, falls within astronomical time. The possibility of self-denial is grounded in the realization that "the real Now-moment" is for the soul "eternity's day." He thus warns, "As long as one clings to time, space, number, and quantity, he is on the wrong track and God is strange and thus far away."[14] The self-emptiness of poverty is God's fullness. The transtemporal and transspatial nature of this fullness becomes apparent in the penultimate words of the Sermon: "God does not first need to enter the person who is already free of all otherness and creature nature, because he is already there."[15] The paradoxical nature of this assertion is only an apparent one, and then only against the background of a cultural perspective in which space and time are regarded as fundamental.

I venture the judgment that what Eckhart sees as the problem of moral action within the Western Augustinian tradition—namely, the will separated in time from the willed—is indeed the fundamental problematic of Western Christianity and the source of its distinctive phenomenon, the "plagued conscience." The problem lies not in the nature of the will, as though it were corrupt, but in the temporalization of the will which separated Intention from Act. The Western insistence upon doing what is paradoxical, that is, what is unintelligible, is the source of the "plagued conscience." And it is Eckhart who saw more clearly than anyone else in the West that the paradox arises from a false weighting of temporality. The theory of Pure Experience with its complementary notion of the relational

---

[13]Blakney, *Meister Eckhart*, 212.

[14]Ibid., 213.

[15]Ibid., 214.

self[16] has the potential for dissolving the paradox in a way which is fully commensurate with Eckhart's vision. The concept of relational selfhood affords a reconceptualization of temporality which makes reaccessing "Good" a reality.

The Conceptual Detemporalizing of the Will as the *Sine Qua Non* for Reaccessing "Good"

When Nishida's early work, *A Study of Good,* was first brought to my attention by Fritz Buri in 1976, I felt there was a strangeness about the title; surely it should have read *A Study of the Good.* As I became more aware of its profound content, I realized the fundamental difference between "Good" and "the Good." The latter is a transcendentalized object, rendered ultimately inaccessible by the temporalization of the will. The former, "Good," on the contrary, *is* accessible for the simple reason that in Pure Experience "there is not the slightest interval between the demands and the realization of the will."[17] Either "Good" *is* (that is, is immediate) or it *is* not. And it *is* where no conceptual temporal separation intrudes between Intention and Act. Wherever and whenever any conceptual interval does intrude, then "Good" is transfigured into "the Good," that is, into an elusive impossible possibility.

The fundamental correlation between moral action and atemporality is by and large foreign to Western Christianity. Eckhart is virtually unique in this regard. If one surveys other religious traditions for one that is sensitive to this correlation, the principal candidate that presents itself is Zen Buddhism. I have elsewhere defended the thesis that the Zen doctrine of No-Mind is isomorphic with the deepest meaning of Christian self-denial.[18] In neither does

---

[16]For a more extensive treatment of the notions of Pure Experience and the "relational self," cf. essay 3, above.

[17]Nishida Kitaro, *A Study of Good,* trans. V. H. Viglielmo (1960) 6.

[18]Cf. essay 3, above, 42-44.

a moral "subject" *produce* the action. Such a claim will undoubtedly fall on deaf ears in the West, where individualism may be stronger than anywhere else on the globe. To that audience I have tried to make moral action intelligible by offering a relational theory of experience, many of whose central features were articulated in part one of this present essay. I shall now return to that paradigm of experience for the purpose of applying it to moral action.

If Immediacy is all there is, then "Good" is immediate or it *is* not, that is, it is but an idea or ideal—an abstraction in any case. If it is immediate, then it participates fully in reality. That means that in immediate moral action (there being no other) no moral "subject" produces the action, for the notion of "subject" arises only through the reflective analysis of Immediacy, that is, through mediation. Hence there is no occasion within Immediacy for moral pride of achievement or moral despair over failure. It follows that such emotions arise only where moral action is conceived as the act of a fundamental subject. Since the tradition of Western Christianity habitually conceived the nature of moral action along the pattern I have just enunciated, I am compelled to draw upon other traditions to illustrate the morality of Immediacy. Frequently I cite Eugen Herrigel's classic, *Zen in the Art of Archery*, as a prime example of a relational view of experience. In his account of his laborious attempt to master the "technique" of Zen archery, the sense of what *is* and what *is not* appears in the Zen master's remark, hopelessly enigmatic to most Westerners, that the bowstring must go through your thumb.[19] Here is the practical sense of Nishida's profound moral insight that "there is not the slightest interval between the demands and the realization of the will."

I do not think we are forced finally to "turn to the East" to find such an insight. In my opinion, it is fully present in the Christian injunction to self-denial, however blind to its deepest meaning we in Western Christianity have continued to be.

---

[19]Eugen Herrigel, *Zen in the Art of Archery*, with an introduction by D. T. Suzuki, trans. R. F. C. Hull (1971).

By the norms of Western Christianity the relational theory of moral action seems vulnerable to the charge that the moral category of responsibility, that is, of personal accountability, is lost. I should reply that in the West the category of "oughtness" has been defined in accordance with its temporalized notion of will and selfhood. If Kant's moral question, "What ought I (to) do?", is taken at face value, there results a conceptual separation of the "is" from the "ought"; for the "ought" of his query *is* not (at least, not yet), but *to be*. This is certainly the ground of the Western claim that moral intention is not moral action. Its notion of "the Good" entails the notion of what ought "to be." "Good," on the contrary, always *is*. The fundamental moral question consonant with this ontology of Good is then, not Kant's question, "What should I do?", but rather the query, "Is this present action 'Good'?" Some may ask what possible meaning can be given to "Good" in this question. Our religious heritage is univocal on this matter: "Love one another"; "the greatest of these is love"; "God is love." According to the fundamental meaning of our tradition, Love is not one relationship among other relationships, but rather the supreme paradigm of the fundamentality of relatedness, that is, of the constitutive character of relation. Love is not something *we* do; it is rather what *defines* who we are. "Love is the fulfilling of the law": where there is love, there is "Good." Where there is no love, there is no "Good."

One of the finest affirmations of this central religious insight to be found in modern literature appears in Stendahl's work cited at the beginning of this essay. Although the title under which he discusses the insight contrasts love with integrity, it is clear that in a final sense they are not disjunctive. Speaking more specifically of "charity," Stendahl expresses an idea fully commensurate with the thesis of this present essay: "[Charity] does not work for the simple reason that it is not 'love' as long as the ego (collective or individual, we/I) wants to remain in command, wants to call the shots, to be in control. True love demands that neither the giver nor the receiver be conscious of giving or receiving."[20]

---

[20]Stendahl, *Paul among Jews and Gentiles*, 56.

The thesis offered in this present essay stands as a challenge to Cobb's thesis that Judeo-Christianity was characterized by the quest for a second ultimate, the principle of rightness. In view of the interpretation of moral action developed in my essay I offer the suggestion that the principle he defines as the second ultimate applies properly, not to Judeo-Christian experience as imaged in Scripture, but to the alteration of that legacy in Western Christianity. If such a claim is viable, it follows that in their root traditions, Buddhism and Judeo-Christianity share in the affirmation of a single ultimate. For there can be but one ultimate.

6 | Relational Metaphysics and the Human Future

The complexity of the question of the human future is such that all proposals for redirecting human energies towards the actualization of value seem utterly simplistic. Radical pessimism produces prophets of doom; extreme optimism produces preachers of utopia. Most of the world's sages fall somewhere between these extremes, convinced of the worth and dignity of life despite human evidence to the contrary, and fully expectant that humanity has the natural endowment necessary to redeem the tragic, at least partially.

There is very little triumphalism left in the West. Gone are the old religious and humanistic liberals who proclaimed the gospel of irreversible progress in late nineteenth-century Europe and early twentieth-century America. The harshness of defeat left a cultural crisis of the first magnitude in Germany after World War I; the ideological crises surrounding racism, terrorism, ecological deterioration, nuclear arms proliferation, and the morality and futility of war deeply eroded the vestiges of "manifest destiny" still felt in the

United States even after World War II. The ideal of "One World" held out by some as an imminent *pax aeterna* turned out to be as morally and politically ambiguous as the idea of nationhood has proved to be in the modern World. The religious message of the Kingdom of God survived with considerable vitality through many of the radical and unexpected technological and political novelties of modern society, but seems now to be completely immobilized, a victim of societal complexification. The great ethical systems of the past, philosophical and religious, were formulated in a simpler time and now seem to many to be adequate only for simple times. Something of the mood of our times is captured in a recent advertising line from a modern industrial enterprise: "There are no simple solutions. Only intelligent choices."[1]

National ideologies which for centuries have provided a cultural womb of security and identity have been challenged by global ideologies which promise a new transnational security and identity. But these global gospels have lost their credibility to the degree that their means have proved to be subhuman. Even the phenomenon of ideology has lost its revolutionary power, a victim of the redeeming human proclivity for dialogue. The truly resolute have become very few, and the fewer they are, the more desperate they become, especially when their resolve has ideological roots.

The international mood is ripe for cultural despair, a globalization of Spengler's *Kulturpessimismus*. It has assumed many modern forms: resignation to cultural pluralism, rampant personal and cultural disorientation, senseless acts of political and ideological terrorism, and the frightening realization that human consumption is fast outstripping the known resources.

During the past decade a complete rethinking of individual, cultural, and global priorities was initiated with a view to providing realistic alternatives to what has seemed to some to be a disaster course for humankind. Massive quests for new energies, new food

---

[1]Caterpillar Tractor Company advertisement, *National Geographic Magazine* 150 (July 1976) 1.

sources and ecologically viable life-styles for nations and persons have been undertaken. Masses of persons are turning to the occult, the psychic, and—in the West—to Oriental mysticism for a personal and social wholeness not provided in established social institutions, the lack of which has been the cause of much personal disorientation. Increased energies and fiscal resources are being poured into the quest for contact with "extra-terrestrial intelligence" in the hope that some meaning may be restored to human existence in the face of the current "centerless cosmos" of modern cosmology and astrophysics. There are today forms of hope never before imagined: cryogenic resurrection, organ-transplant technology, the founding of space communities, the discovery and elimination of the physiological causes of aging, to name only a few. While the production of global utopias has not been revived in the old classical style, the quest for individual and societal salvation has come to dominate the lives of many persons in the modern world. Whether that salvation is sought in dietary experimentation, in vigorous exercise, in meditation, in evangelical fervor or in technologically more complex forms of leisure, it is sought with all the rigor and abandon of the religious seekers of older times.

Since salvation has always proved to be more of a "hope" than a reality, it is appropriate in an essay on hope to probe the grounds of this human preoccupation with the length and quality of life. I should like to propose that a distinction be made between the human conditions that generate the passion for future-directed life, on the one hand, and the dimensions of experience that supply the form and content of convincing individual and social gospels on the other. The former, the situational conditions for refocusing life towards the future, is best summed up in the word *despair*. While etymologically it simply designates the lack of hope, socially it designates a fundamental not-having that becomes a not-being. While my reservations about Ernst Bloch's *Prinzip-Hoffnung* are a matter of public record,[2] I am the first to admit the impressiveness of his insight that

---

[2]Harold H. Oliver, "Hope and Knowledge: The Epistemic Status of Religious Language," *Cultural Hermeneutics* 2 (1974) 75-78.

hope arises out of a lack, a *horror vacui*, that cries for fulfilling. According to Bloch, driven philosophically by the economic vision of the theories of Marx, the fundamental *horror vacui* is *hunger.* Bloch develops a comprehensive social vision of hope out of a systematic phenomenological analysis of this most natural and threatening lack—the lack of food. There is no denying the ideological passion of Bloch's phenomenology of hope, though most of us are aware that since the time he wrote his *opus classicum* on hope in Cambridge, Massachusetts, in the 1940s, the problem of meeting the world's physical needs is no longer the simple issue of the means of production. There are the almost insurmountable related issues of pollution of foodstuffs and air, the foretold end of fossil fuels, and world inflation that always falls most heavily on the truly poor. I realize that Bloch only uses hunger as a phenomenological instrument, and that his major focus is on the quality of life in a larger sense. He is more concerned with the dehumanizing of life which the capitalistic solution to the meeting of human needs has produced—as, for example, in the Industrial Revolution—than he is with logistical problems of production and distribution, and this is appropriate for a social philosopher and theoretician.

Bloch is correct to point out that hope arises out of despair, that is, out of the desperation of persons who are experiencing some fundamental lack. When this lack is seen as the by-product of religious, economic, or political conspiracy, it is rightly interpreted by the "have-nots" as oppression, and the form hope then takes is some gospel of liberation. The apocalyptic texts produced by Jews and Christians living under Roman rule comprise such a gospel. The unwritten but passionately sung spirituals of American slaves announced liberation. And the new theologies of liberation reflect the cultural desperation of Afro-Americans, feminists, ethnic minorities, and Third World peoples. The degree of passion with which any gospel is accepted is a measure of the depth of the despair to which it addresses itself. Moreover, gospels are iconoclastic; they denounce the present to bring about a better future.

In exploring aspects of the conditions that lead persons and societies to direct their lives to what is "not-yet," I certainly do not wish to give the impression that what I shall have to say about the human future will measure up where others have fallen short. The complexity of the question of the human future, to which I referred in the opening sentence, should serve as a sober caveat to any social dreamer. The relational schema I shall set forth in the following pages is attended by the conviction that it may meet a deeply felt need in our times to which I have not yet given attention, namely, the feeling of despair arising from the inadequacy of prevailing theories of reality to account for what we experience. I should like to thematize this phenomenon of modern life under the heading:

Conceptual Origins of Modern Despair

The subdivision of world history into distinct periods often follows fundamental shifts in worldview, as for example, in the distinction of the Medieval from the Modern Period in the West. The emergence of any radically new way of conceiving reality has usually entailed both a new sense of what is the case, and an iconoclastic judgment upon a prevailing paradigm of reality. The modern era in the West signalled the discovery of the modern subject and a negative evaluation of medieval introspection. With the subjectivity came *pari passu* the notion of "objects" (*Gegenstände*), of an objective world "over against the subject" which is at the subject's disposal. Here lie the origins of modern scientific objectivity, as well as of modern psychology. The conceptual by-products are present at all levels of our modern Western culture: Idealism and Realism in philosophy, with their opposing claims of the reality of the subject-world and of the object-world, respectively; Transcendence and Behaviorism, with their opposing claims of the fundamentality of the spiritual and the psychophysical realms, respectively; and Theism and Naturalism, with their rival claims about which is ultimate, God or Nature.

These modern Western options may seem *prima facie* to be academic and removed from daily life, but further reflection should indicate that they have in fact pervaded our culture, determining the being and well-being of most of us as we make personal decisions, conduct our professions, decide what to do with our wealth and make commitments of time. I venture the judgment that these conceptual options are to a large degree responsible for our psychic moods, both good and ill. The modern asocial self—the extreme version of individual subjectivity—may well underlie the psychic disorders of our time which are signalled by the growing dependence upon mind-stabilizing drugs and psychotherapy. Modern psychotherapy is, like all modern sciences, a function of modern possibilities; but it can also be said that it came into being to deal with the modern subject, a truly new phenomenon in human history. The diagnosis of psychic ills follows the concept of the psyche current in a given culture. In societies where the psyche is conceived reciprocally, psychic disorder means the loss of social viability; in other societies where the psyche is conceived individualistically, psychic ills are diagnosed as derangement, that is, as loss of inner composure. In our modern Western society predominantly informed by modern subjectivism, the latter idea prevails. While it is the function of psychiatrists to effect personal diagnoses in accord with the prevailing paradigm by which psychic order is defined, it is the task of philosophers oriented to metaphysical questions to arbitrate the larger issue of the viability of prevailing paradigms of personal and societal well-being.

I have chosen to focus upon conceptual origins of despair because of my conviction that conceptual paradigms lie at the root of a culture's well-being or disorder. Since the notion of despair has been defined primarily as a lack or inadequacy of some kind, it is appropriate to assume that the conceptual categories selected for special mention below are ways of viewing reality which I have judged to be inadequate in some final sense. The conceptual categories I wish to discuss include the prevailing notions of ontology, ethics, and religion.

The Inadequacy of Prevailing Options in Ontology

An ontology is a systematic statement of what is fundamental. It selects from the infinite variety of experiences those features or components that are fundamental to any experience whatsoever. In everyday discourse we do not always make such distinctions, the result being that our first encounters with such rigorous statements are characterized by unbelief. Those who do make these distinctions out of ordinary "everyday" experiences often find their judgments about what is fundamental to be inadequate for experiences that are "below" (micro-) or "above" (macro-) the physical and social dimensions of what I have called "the middle range of the empirical." Such persons often retain their "everyday"-ontologies for the interpretation of the experiences from which they were derived, and turn to specialized ontologies for the interpretation of special experiences. For example, there are persons who use a special ontology for interpreting their quantum mechanical research, a different special ontology for their interpretation of macrocosmic events and dimensions, and perhaps even a completely different special ontology to interpret their mystical experiences. While such persons may experience some discomfort due to the radical discontinuities of their separate ontologies, they are certainly likely to be less frustrated than others who try to extend *intact* their singular ontology based upon "the middle range of the empirical" to experiences which are "below" or "above" that range. The desperate efforts of some physicists to defend a "classical" interpretation of quantum phenomena illustrates the difficulty of the former, while John Wisdom's famous "tale" of the Gardener[3] seriously threatens the propriety of the latter.

---

[3]John Wisdom, "Gods," originally published in *Proceedings of the Aristotelian Society* (1944); reprinted in his *Philosophy and Psychoanalysis* (New York: Philosophical Library, 1953) 149-68. The tale of the gardener is found in the latter publication on 154ff. Antony Flew developed this "tale" into the so-called "Parable of the Gardener" in his contribution to the university debate published as chapter 6 in Antony Flew and Alasdair MacIntyre, eds., *New Essays in Philosophical The-*

Prior cultural events have deeply affected the ways we think about reality in the West. The formation of all modern Western languages was such that it is virtually inevitable for Westerners to take their cues for what is fundamental from the linguistic structures of their language. Since these languages all embody a subject-predicate structure with the predication primarily announcing temporality, it was inevitable that persons who speak these languages should assign fundamentality to subjects, objects, and time. These three notions, plus the related notion of space, have all been accorded the status of reality at various times in the West. The classical Newtonian theory of the world made time and space absolute, much to the regret of his contemporary, Leibniz, who regarded them as having only ideality. Newton's theory was operationally so successful that it was an impetus to the Age of Reason whose most representative ontology was that of Mechanistic Materialism. Newton has but one equal in terms of the role he played in shaping Western thought, and that was Descartes who laid the foundations for modern subjectivity. The long Augustinian tradition in the Western Church, not always determinative of Catholic thought, can be credited with having played a major role in creating the conditions for Descartes's instantaneous success. The establishing of the certainty of the *cogito* would, however, be costly; for the inevitable consequence would be uncertainty about the ontological status of the *cogitatum*. It was Immanuel Kant who would address this problem of the "objectivity of the object"[4] in such a fundamental way that, as a consequence, subsequent Western philosophy would be dominated by the subject-object problematic wherever Kant's influence prevailed. The Cartesian-Kantian axis in Western philosophy determined that, thereafter, ontologies in the West would focus pri-

---

ology, The Library of Philosophy and Theology (London: SCM Press, 1955) cf. esp. 96-97

[4]Martin Heidegger, *What is a Thing?*, trans. W. B. Barton, Jr. and Vera Deutsch, with an analysis by Eugene T. Gendlin, Gateway edition (Chicago: Henry Regnery Co., 1967) 55.

marily upon the problem of certainty, and that means the problem of knowing with certainty. For anyone committed to Descartes as a starting point it was the reality of the "known" rather than of the "knower" that would be problematic. In this way the subjectivist bias of modern Western philosophy was established. Its most articulate expression appeared in the form of Modern Idealism according to which reality is mental. It reached its apex in Absolute Idealism with its notion of the Pure Ego composing its world. Once Descartes's assumptions were accepted as a point of departure, it was inevitable that the notion of the absolute subject would eventually arise. Modern Western individualism and egoism owe their origins largely to these events. Although few persons bother to trace this legacy to its roots, Western values and life-styles are predominantly informed by the notions of subject and subjectivity that began with Descartes and received classical form at the hands of Kant. Idealism continues as one of the most respectable ontologies among Western metaphysicians.

Until rather recently, the only serious alternative to Idealism advocated in the West was Realism (or Materialism) which simply rejects the priority of the subject as a way of accommodating the objective reality of the world. Realism has its roots, oddly enough, in Medieval Nominalism which accorded ideas the status of abstractions, in contrast to the Realists of the time for whom the notions were judged to be fundamental. As would be imagined, for modern realists the problem of uncertainty surrounds the status of the subject, and various schools within the movement are distinguished by their diverse judgments on the reality of the subject-world.

My concern in relating these details is threefold: (1) to show that Western philosophy has made available only two major options, Idealism and Realism, which are polar opposites; (2) to establish for later consideration that these historic options are both variants of the same fundamental assumption, not always admitted, namely, that reality must be sought within a subject-object frame of reference. Idealism and Realism represent absolutizations of these polar aspects, respectively. (3) My final concern is more basic to the task

I have set for myself in his essay: I want to suggest that modern Western life is so fundamentally interpenetrated with these options that few exercise the imagination needed to suggest radically new ways of conceiving reality. Moreover, the fact that so many psychological, social, economic and political ills of our culture are rooted in these one-sided options makes it all the more urgent that more holistic ontologies be proposed. Masses of people in the West are turning away from the traditional cultural options in search of more adequate ontologies; for the one common element underlying the current preoccupation with the occult, the psychic, and Eastern spirituality is the desire for holistic alternatives to the predominantly analytic modes of Western thought. My conviction is that the Western cultural heritage has a tradition of holism which can and should be developed and made available to those in the West who are disaffected with current assumptions about reality.

The Inadequacy of Prevailing Options in Ethics

However much professional philosophers and ethicists may question the propriety of deriving the ought from the is, it is a cultural fact that current Western notions of morality are grounded in accepted notions about what is real. I for one find this state of affairs fully justifiable, although my judgment stands that the historic ontological commitments in the West are woefully inadequate.

The absolutization of the subject in some forms of Modern Idealism has served to transcendentalize "Good," that is, to make it into a mere regulative concept, "the Good." Another way of stating this claim is to say that morality is temporalized, in that a temporal interval is established, conceptually, between Intention and Act. In other essays I have spoken of this distinctive feature of Western ethics as "the temporalization of the will."[5] Just as subjectivist ontology introduced a (spatial) interval between "knower" and "known," making the latter a transcendental object, so its notion of

---

[5]Cf. essays 3 and 4, above.

moral action makes "Good" remote and inaccessible. For the intrusion of a temporal interval so isolates intention that it has become proverbial in the West to denigrate so-called "good intentions."

The personal and social by-products of this morality of "the Good" are obsessive guilt on one hand, and an inordinate sense of subjective achievement on the other. In a society where individualism is the most determinate form of existence the "subject-self" of its ontology becomes "the Moral Ego" of its ethics.

Where Realism constitutes the ontology, the epistemic status of selfhood is made problematic. In certain political ideologies, which are variants of Realism or Materialism, the self is even trivialized by being reduced to the status of other "objective things." To the extent that modern forms of humanism presuppose a realistic ontology, the morality they advocate is grounded in pragmatic considerations. Even so, the pervasive power of Western subjectivism is such that the realists generally assume with the idealists that Intention is temporally separate from Act. It is for this reason that one speaks justifiably of the subjectivist bias of modern Western culture. One has only to compare Asian and Oriental cultures to realize the extent of that subjectivist bias.

The Inadequacy of Prevailing Religious Options

The plasticity of ancient religious traditions has been demonstrated throughout world history. The vitality of religion within modern secular states is phenomenal, especially when one considers how vastly different the modern cultural matrix is from those ancient cultures in which religions were given traditional form. Rather than dying the death "of a thousand qualifications" as predicted by analytic philosophers, Western theism seems more virulent than ever before, just at a time when non-Western religions are on the rise in the West.

Religion appears to be an ineradicable component in human identity, but is it always benign? The most cursory acquaintance with human history will convince one that religion has been a "mixed blessing" in virtually all cultures, modern culture being no excep-

tion. Nevertheless, religious institutions, practices, and beliefs per-
dure through cultural upheavals; one reason for this, sociologically
speaking, may be the almost universal willingness to cite human
frailty rather than the inadequacy of current religious ideals when
adherents of a religion malign or manipulate each other or "out-
siders" in the name of their deity(-ies).

While it would be presumptuous to speak of the West as "Christian," it is certainly the case that Christianity is a Western religion.
It arose in the West and has never made significant inroads into non-
Western cultures. It is also the case that no other religion (Judaism
and Islam are special cases) has had any significant success in the
West. The fact that Western peoples and their cultures have never
been at peace with themselves or with others was justified theolog-
ically by Luther who characterized a Christian as *simul justus et
peccator*.

The apocalyptic origins of Christianity determined that this
emergent out of Judaism would be a religion of hope of very speci-
fiable content. The success of Christianity in originally pagan European cultures must be explained in part by the fact that it was
equipped with the most powerful ideological weapon—the promise
of everlasting life. In subsequent eras of depravity and deprivation
Christian eschatological belief has surfaced with unusual power. An
eschatological orientation is so fundamental to Christianity that the
most universal of all negative evaluations placed upon that religion
has been its "otherworldliness." As in other religions, so in Christianity, the grounds of its strength have been the sources of its
weakness.

Christianity is not a simple phenomenon; it is present in the
West in a multiplex form. Its diversity follows cultural, geographic,
linguistic, and even regional divisions, and these overlap with other
distinctions of intra- and inter-Church doctrine and practice. Even
so, Western Christianity is unified through a doctrine of personhood that informs not only its confessed followers, but those "without" as well. Eastern Orthodox Christianity represents a
wholesome exception. Christian personhood as defined today has

both informed and been informed by Western subjectivism. Radical individualism has so thoroughly come to define Western Christian personhood that the latter's fundamental teaching of "self-denial" is either trivialized by its followers or regarded as so paradoxical as to be irrelevant.

Its unholy alliance with subjectivism in its modern form has rendered Christian faith impotent to cope with the psychic and social ills arising from subjectivist ontology. Can the fact that Christians experience psychic disorientation and deterioration as fully as non-Christians also be laid at the door of human frailty? I should like to suggest, to the contrary, that it is Christianity *as presently conceived* that is at fault. There are many ways of conceiving the meaning of Christian faith, some of which have already proved their inadequacy in times past. What is it about the present conception that makes present-day Christianity more a part of the problem than of the solution? I hasten to venture the judgment that what plagues modern Christianity is a conceptual inadequacy. Its conceptual inadequacy is largely an ontological one, resulting from its alliance with subjectivism. The consequence is that Christians fall victim to all the ills accompanying subjectivist ontology, but—what is even more tragic—they fall victim as well to other anxieties uniquely endemic to any subjectivist version of theistic belief. A serious look at the dynamic of theism versus atheism in Western culture should suffice to illustrate this problem.

Within prereflective mythic awareness what we later call theism represents an affirmation of divine-human relatedness, that is, of the co-reality of the I and the Thou. It is the form through which the ancient religious imagination gave expression to its fundamental sense of reality. In the narrative world of myth this affirmation of relatedness is "character-ized," that is, it is dramatically developed through characters-in-relation. Their independent reality, that is, their existence *outside* the drama, is of no concern to the text. My hermeneutical theory of myth is that myths—stories of the gods—are most faithfully interpreted in a *relational* way, that is, as affirmations of the fundamentality of relatedness.

Since the rise of modern Rationalism a different hermeneutical paradigm has been in effect. The rationalists took the myths to be *cognitively referential* but denied the reality of their "referents." Defenders of the faith responded by claiming the reality of those "referents," that is, by insisting that the stories were true, little realizing that they, by becoming defenders, had undergone a hermeneutical transformation of the first magnitude. For they had succumbed to rationalistic *referential* hermeneutics; whatever had remained until that time of prereflective mythic awareness was exchanged—by the faithful—for a biblical literalism that owed its possiblity to rationalism.

The importance of that development for the present problem of the inadequacy of modern Western religiosity should be readily apparent. Rationalism created both theism and atheism in the modern sense by the same gambit; for Modern Theism—the assertion of the existence of the Wholly Other—is understandable only as a counter-assertion to Modern Atheism. In the pre-differentiated world of mythic awareness neither claim makes any sense.

The Church became the cultural bastion of modern theism, while its members became potential victims of reasonable doubt about the external reality of the divine beings *referred to* in its doctrinal and liturgical heritage. The *cogitatum* methodically placed in doubt by Descartes, to whom it did not occur to include the Deity, became inexorably inclusive of all transcendent beings. Doubt became an obsessive way of life in the West, both "within" and "without" the community of the faithful. For those "within," it adulterated the innocence of simple faith; for those "without," it became the ultimate justification for their nonalliance. Those who are truly "outside" have a measure of tranquillity not experienced by those whose faith is complicated by its uneasy contract with an alien hermeneutic. For these persons the original substance of the Christian hope is transformed into what in modern times has been called "the eschatological argument," that is, into the expectation that the certainty of what is believed will come at the end of the journey. Belief is exhaustively transfigured into hope, but the "object" of hope becomes the eschatological verification of the "external referents" of belief. Hope becomes a form of despair. Only those who have experienced the anxiety attendant upon this debilitating state of affairs can appreciate its ultimate inadequacy. Later I shall outline an ontology developed as an alternative to the current subjectivist and objectivist ontologies, and will then indicate its significance for the residual role of religion in modern culture.

What sources of hope are available to Western folk who experience anxiety and disorientation due to inadequate conceptual options in ontology, morality, and religion? Hope by its very nature is a protest against a lack, a deficiency, a nonfulfilment. Eschatological inversion is its classic Christian content; conceptual inversion is the needed modern response to despair arising from conceptual inadequacies.

Modern Sources of Hope:
Radically New Reconceptualizations
of Reality, Temporality, Morality, and Religion

It should be apparent by this point that ontology, temporality, morality, and religion are not separate issues, but are conceptually interwoven in the deepest way imaginable. Though the topics must appear seriatim, every effort will be made to show their theoretical and practical interconnection.

A Relational Theory of Reality:
Reality Is Relatedness

Idealism and Realism represent aspectual absolutizations of the subject-predicate paradigm, respectively. While the viability of this paradigm was not questioned seriously until the rise of phenomenology, the grounds for choice within its limits were routinely discussed under the topic of internal versus external relations. The three major modern positions taken in this debate were: (1) that all relations are external; (2) that all relations are internal; and (3) that some relations are external, some internal. Using the formula, aRb, we may say that position (1) takes the *relata* as fundamental, the relation as contingent. Position (2) takes the *relata* as ontologically defined by the relation. The final theory holds (1) to be the case for certain relations, (2) for others. Few modern philosophers have agreed with Bertrand Russell in holding all relations to be external, in that the unity of experience seems inexplicable on these terms. Bradley and his colleagues, including Brand Blanshard, have based their monism on the doctrine of the fundamentality of relations, a position its opponent, Charles Hartshorne, appropriately labels "The Thesis of Universal Internality." G. E. Moore, Hartshorne, and his mentor, Whitehead, are the names usually thought of in connection with the view that some relations are external, some internal. It is certainly beyond dispute that any ontology that claims the fundamentality of process would necessarily support this latter position on relations.[6]

Relational metaphysics assumes the thesis of universal internality and rigorously carries through its implications with a

---

[6]Bertrand Russell's view was set forth in his *Principles of Mathematics*, second edition reprint (New York: W. W. Norton Co., 1938; first published in 1903) 100; he reiterated his position in "The Monistic Theory of Truth," in his *Philosophical Essays*, reprint (New York: Simon and Shuster, 1966; first published in 1910) 131-46. G. E. Moore's historic essay on relations is available in his *Philosophical Studies* (Totowa NJ: Littlefield, Adams and Co., 1968) cf. esp. 276-308. Charles Hartshorne's defense of the asymmetry of relations is a principal feature of many of his publications, including *Man's Vision of God and The Logic of Theism* (New York: Harper and Row, 1953; first published in 1941) 326; *The Divine Relativity: A Social Conception of God* (New Haven: Yale University Press, 1948) esp. 62-67, 103-14; and *Creative Synthesis and Philosophic Method* (London: SCM Press, 1970) esp. 52ff., 84ff., 99-119, 210-23. F. H. Bradley's classic statement in favor of internality was set forth in the appendix to his *Appearance and Reality* (Oxford: Clarendon Press, 1893) esp. in 512-22. His view was defended and expanded by Brand Blanshard, *The Nature of Thought* (New York: Macmillan Co., 1940) 449-91; and more recently in his article "Internal Relations and Their Importance to Philosophy," *Review of Metaphysics* 21 (1967): 227-36. Since Alfred North Whitehead gives no extensive treatment of relations *per se*, I shall here simply concede to the "scholastics" that Hartshorne faithfully represents his mentor's position.

view to effecting a generalization of experience. Absolute rigor in the application of this assumption leads to the conclusion that *a* and *b* represent "functional dependencies" (Cassirer's term)[7] of the relating, *R*. Idealism is grounded in the assumption of the fundamentality of *a*, the "subject"; Realism, in the assumption of the fundamentality of some *b*'s, that is, of those "objects" that have a physical reference. Relationalism is based on the thesis that *all* and *only* relations are fundamental. It further argues that any and all ontologies based on the fundamentality of the *relata* commit the "fallacy of misplaced concreteness" (Whitehead's term).[8] The extreme relational thesis could be falsely interpreted to mean that the *relata* are unreal, that is, illusory. According to my relational metaphysical scheme, the *relata* are mere abstractions; they are derivatives of fundamentals whose emergence is explained by the instrument I call *biperspectivism* (a term I learned from Ervin Laszlo).[9] As applied to relations, it means that when any relation is viewed *ingressively*, the notion of the subject emerges; when viewed *effectively*, the notion of the object appears.[10] Thus any action (*R*) has the possibility of such co-derivatives. Since all Western languages are

---

[7]Ernst Cassirer, "Einstein's Theory of Relativity," in his *Substance and Function and Einstein's Theory of Relativity* (New York: Dover Publications, 1953; first published in 1921) 379.

[8]This characteristic Whiteheadian phrase appeared in his *Science and the Modern World, Lowell Lectures, 1925* (New York: The Free Press, 1967; first published in 1925) cf., e.g., 51 and 58; and in his *Process and Reality: An Essay in Cosmology* (New York: Harper and Brothers, 1960; first published in 1929) cf. 11 and 27.

[9]Ervin Laszlo, *Introduction to Systems Philosophy*, Harper Torchbooks edition (New York: Harper and Row, 1972) 154.

[10]The terms "ingressively" and "effectively" are borrowed from Greek grammatical usage where they function to distinguish nuances of the aorist tense. The fact that the "aorist" expressed "undefined action" gave rise to the grammatical theory that one using it may have, under certain circumstances, intended to stress either the incipient character of the act (hence "ingressive") or the act viewed in terms of its result (hence "effectively").

structured in the subject-predicate form, it is in the West that there
has been the greatest tendency to reify these *relata*. Since it is
somewhat easier to show how these two idioms (that is, relational
and subject-object) emerged by appeal to the philosophical notion of
Pure Experience, I shall now turn to this latter idiom. I should say
in advance that I judge the theory of Pure Experience to be a variant
version of the relational scheme already set forth.

The adjective "pure" in the notion, "Pure Experience," means
"prior to reflection." In Pure Experience, there is only Immediacy,
Pure Activity. There is no "subject," no "object," no "prior" and no
"posterior." There is only the Now-Moment, lacking differentiations
of time, "actors" and "acted upon" (to use terms met earlier in the
discussion of relations). These differentiations emerge through reflection on Pure Experience, which being mediated by reflection is
no longer Immediate. Thus on the model of Pure Experience, subject-selves, objects, and object-selves, past and future, are abstractions rather than concrete entities. The grounds for their
appearance lie not in Pure Experience but in the nature of reflection. Philosophers and theologians of "consciousness" argue that
thinking always implies "thinking subject" and "object thought"; Jaspers, for example, spoke of the "subject-object schema of consciousness." But as even these thinkers have indicated, not all
experience is "cognitive," that is, reflective. The thesis of Pure Experience entails the rejection of the entitivity of consciousness,
holding it too to be an abstraction. "Consciousness," as cognitively
understood, is merely a product of reflection, nothing more.

Drawing upon both of these idioms, relational metaphysics and
Pure Experience, I venture the following ontological conclusions
which are radically significant for modern life. Reality consists not
of "things-in-relation" (that is, *relata*) but of *relations*. By extension,
reality is *relatedness*. And relating is Immediacy, Pure Activity. Neither subject- nor object-selves, nor object-things, are fundamental.
It is appropriate, however, to use the term selfhood, but only in the
form, "the (or a) Relational Self." As I tried to indicate in an earlier
essay[11] the relational self is not the subject-self, is not "located in

---

[11]Cf. essay 3, above.

space and time" and does not calculate its moral worth. It is the self of Pure Experience, of the I-Thou. Those who want to read the purest statements on the notion of the relational self should turn to Zen texts, for there one will find a purity of expression that can only come from centuries of refinement of the notion. Two excerpts from Suzuki's phenomenal article, "The Zen Doctrine of No-Mind," should suffice to illustrate the insight from that tradition.

> When thus the seeing of self-nature has no reference to a specific state of consciousness, which can be logically or relatively defined as a something, the Zen masters designate it in negative terms and call it 'no-thought' or 'no-mind', wu-nien or wu-hsin. As it is "no-thought" or "no-mind," the seeing is really the seeing.[12]

and

> The state of no-mind-ness refers to the time prior to the separation of mind and world, when there is yet no mind standing against an external world and receiving its impressions through the various sense-channels. Not only a mind, but a world, has not yet come into existence.[13]

While such ontological notions may seem utterly strange and inscrutable to the Western mind, I have tried to indicate that there are Western options which are isomorphic with them, such as Pure Experience. It would seem to follow that Eastern and Western conceptual interchange is not just some passing fad, but is absolutely crucial to the *bene esse* of Western self-perception.

A Relational Theory of Temporality: toward a Phenomenology of "Futurity"

Ontological, ethical and eschatological considerations make it imperative that I treat the problem of temporality and experience in some detail. Classical physics strongly influenced Western philosophy to accept the fundamentality of linear time; considerable in-

---

[12]William Barrett, ed., *Zen Buddhism. Selected Writings of D. T. Suzuki*, Anchor Books edition (New York: Doubleday, 1956) 163.

[13]Ibid., 219.

centives toward that move had long been provided by the temporalization of history and eschatology in Western theology from the time of Augustine. Peoples who are ideologically non-Western, such as Orientals and native Americans, commonly view Western culture as distinguished by its linear sense of history. It should have come as no shock when I located the distinctive problematic of Western morality in its temporalization of the Will. The "phenomenology of futurity" soon to be explicated will result in an alternative interpretation of moral existence. As for eschatology, the third consideration mentioned above, the relational theory of reality and temporality should issue in a recovery of the reality of hope.

From the perspective of relational metaphysics time and space are treated as derivatives—that is, abstractions—which are characterized as belonging exhaustively to the language and logic of measurement. This relational claim is fully commensurate with the theory of space-time events advanced in the Special Theory of Relativity. In Pure Experience there are no spatio-temporal differentiations, no "prior" or "posterior" to separate "knower" from "known," or Intention from Act. While these spatio-temporal distinctions appear only through reflection, it is faithful to the notion of Pure Experience to speak of Immediacy as having a texture—a texture that includes temporality, but not time in a physical sense. A phenomenology of this temporality will now be undertaken with a view to indicating (1) in what ways it is appropriate to speak temporally of experience, and (2) the experiential conditions out of which Western metaphysics developed its questionable claim for the fundamentality of time.

A Phenomenology of Temporality. Pure Experience is a Now-Moment, but its texture may include a sense of pastness and a sense of futurity. There is a "pastness" of the present (Immediacy) which upon reflection is called "the Past"; there is a "futurity" of the present (Immediacy) which upon reflection becomes "the Future." We experience neither "the Past" nor "the Future"; rather, the reality of the Past is only the experiential "pastness" of the Present, the reality of the "Future" is only the experiential "futurity" of the present. Ontologically speaking, to the extent "the Past" is not "present to us," it is not; to the extent "the Future" is not "present to us," it is not. "The Past" is but the symbolic representation of that aspect of Immediacy we call "pastness"; "the Future" is but the symbolic representation of that aspect of Immediacy we call "futurity." It is only the Present (= Immediacy) that gives the Past; it is only the Present that gives the Future.

Even in ordinary language "the Past" means "what *was*, but *is* no longer *present*"; "the Future" means "what *is* not (yet) *present*." The necessary negations in these statements signal the non-Immediacy, non-presence—hence non-fundamentality—of Past and Future. The word "present" in both formulations is a clue of some importance: the pastness of Immediacy, which gives rise upon reflection to the notion of "the Past," is the experienced "non-presence of what *was* present"; the futurity of Immediacy, which gives rise to the notion of "the Future," is the experienced "non-presence of what *will be* present." Thus in a fundamental way the sense of futurity affirms the Immediacy of Presentness.

Put in another idiom, Pure Experience may include memory and anticipation. Memory is the sense of pastness, the recall of the no longer present; anticipation is the sense of futurity, the present "leaning forward of the present." The reflective reification of memory produces the notion of "the Past"; the reflective reification of anticipation produces the notion of "the Future." Thus "the Past" and "the Future" are mere abstractions, that is, derivatives of what is fundamental. They are not fundamental themselves, for they arise only upon reflection and hence are "mediated" (that is, non-Immediate). And what is non-Immediate is not fundamental.

It follows that there *is* no "Past" and there *is* no "Future." There *is* only pastness; there *is* only futurity. Since the primary concern of this essay is to reestablish legitimate grounds for hope, I shall now attempt to relate hope to the notion of "futurity" rather than of "the Future."

Hope as Present Anticipation. The reality of hope lies in the fact that it is Immediate. An anticipated hope is not yet hope. Hope's reality lies in the fact that it is the *present* anticipation *of something;* it is the *present* negation of a lack in one of the two forms in which a negation of what is present can be real. The other form is memory. Therefore, hope is the actualization of the Not-Yet, the only actuality it *has.* "The Future" has no reality except the reality of "futurity." So far I have spoken of hope from the perspective of a phenomenology of futurity. Now it is imperative to speak phenomenologically about *hope* itself.

Hope is, ontologically speaking, present anticipation, which has both formal and material aspects. Formally, hope is always hope "in something." Bloch has taught us that hope is a formal protest against a *lack*, a deficiency. But hope never appears purely formally; materially considered, hope is always specific. Cultural factors account for this specificity; for persons whose experience has been truly transcultural, the cultural particularism of expectations becomes generalized into no less specific, but less particularistic content.

The relational reconceptualization of reality and of temporality proposed in this essay is intended as an option to existing problematic notions of entities, including subject-selves, objects, and object-selves, as well as "the Past" and "the Future." So far I have only been able to speak formally about hope in the light of these relational statements. Toward the end of this essay I shall attempt to indicate what may be learned from this relational approach about the material content of hope. For the present I must refocus attention on the "phenomenology of futurity" in order to indicate the implications of relational ontology for morality.

A Relational Theory of Morality: Reaccessing "Good"

Western morality reaches its highest expression in the notion of "the Good." I indicated earlier that this notion is a reification of "Good"; it is the *mediated* form of the latter. When the ethical focuses on "the Good," it commits itself to what is *not Immediate*, hence is not. "Good" is transformed into an ideal, that is, into what has only ideality; it becomes an abstraction, lacking actuality. The temporalizing of the will, that is, the separation of Intention from Act, is the great de-realizer of "Good." When "Good" is conceptually de-realized, that is, made non-Immediate, there *is* no moral action; for "the moral" either *is*, or it *is* not. "The Good" may be a moral idea, but it has no actuality. "The Good" is no substitute for "Good."

Against the background of Western morality such claims may appear inscrutable. Actually the claim being made is a simple one: the enactment of the ethical is not future, but now, for enactment that is not *being enacted* is not yet (*is not*) enactment. It is not a moral act only to intend the Good, for good intention—separated from Act—does not constitute "Good." Moral prophets have known this throughout human history. They do not urge consideration of "the Good"; rather they warn: "Enact 'Good' Now." They characteristically have no patience with "later," for reality *is now*, or it *is* not. Those who are culturally conditioned by Western notions of morality alone may find this relational notion of the Immediacy of "Good" morally suspect, for that is the general attitude of Westerners toward Zen religiosity which I find commensurate with morality relationally understood. I for one, however, see no other conceptual alternative to the particular moral problems of Western society than the one I have set forth. In my mind it is the only resolution of the problematic of the "plagued conscience" of the West. The separation of "Moral Subject" from the "Moral Act" is fatal to morality; the interval becomes a cosmic abyss, like the Western theoretical distinction in, say, archery between the "hitter" and the "hit." In Zen archery, on the contrary, since the bowstring must go through the archer's thumb, no such distinction exists. [14] The Western theoret-

---

[14] Eugen Herrigel, *Zen in the Art of Archery*, with an introduction by D. T. Suzuki, trans. R. F. C. Hull, Vintage Book edition (New York: Random House, 1971) 31-32.

ical distinction referred to is as fatal to its ontological concepts as to its moral, for the former determine the latter. A relational ontology, which—like Zen—admits of no such distinction, provides for a reaccessing of "Good" in the Western context.

A Relational Theory of Religion: beyond Belief and Unbelief

It was claimed earlier that inadequate Western concepts of the function of religious affirmation often create an "anxiety of faith" that can be as disorienting as that anxiety to which faith intends to respond. The *referential* interpretation of the great religious myths shifts the focus away from the stories to some supposed transcendent realm, with its transcendent beings, and for this reason alone fails to respect the narrative limits of the stories. Two consequences fatal to religious tranquillity regularly ensue: (1) the dynamic of the religious life becomes the quest for certainty about the reality of these transcendent entities; and (2) an intracultural debate develops primarily around this question of "certainty" which divides the religious from the nonreligious. In both instances the fundamental affirmation of religion can easily be lost.

Since it was essential to introduce my relational theory of religion earlier to support the thesis of the inadequacy of the prevailing referential theory, I must now reiterate and then expand that statement.

Contrary to the reductionist claims of analytic philosophers and those theologians who tried to make sense of religious discourse by assuming those claims, the relational hermeneutics of such discourse holds it to be *ontological* affirmation. Religious discourse in its originative form is a mythical announcement about reality. The reality of which it speaks is the reality of experience; it is only when a *referential* theory of myth prevails that the claim arises that religious discourse is about some transempirical reality. Since from a relational perspective, experience is all there is, religious discourse is interpreted relationally as a statement about experience. Since its ontological claim is available apart from myth, as for example through metaphysics or even physics, it follows that the uniqueness of mythical affirmation lies not in its content, but in its particularized form. Such a statement about myth does not denigrate the religious affirmation, since it is made with the accompanying realization that the cultural appeal of religion lies in its particularity.

Religion is the affirmation of *relatedness*, for myth images the insight that what is fundamental about experience is not that there exist fundamental entities who enjoy the occasional adventure of relationship, but there *is* only *relatedness*. In the great religious epics the story does not exist to establish the reality of the transexperiential; it exists rather to affirm the co-relational character of experience. The *referential* theory of myth assumes that mutuality is a contingent dimension of divine and human entities; the relational theory, that mutuality is what is fundamental. It would be a gross misunderstanding of the relational theory to interpret it as a denial of the transcendent dimension of the mythical; for myth *qua* myth does not reify the transcendent, but employs it to affirm the reality of relatedness. Thus the truly transcendent dimension of myth is its affirmation that experiential reality is relatedness. No other claim about the transcendent is commensurate with the relational theory of religious discourse. In Judaism the affirmation of relatedness takes the form of the I-Thou paradigm of prayer; in Christianity it takes the form of the God-Man paradigm culturally informed by Hellenistic-Oriental piety. Metaphysically considered, these religious paradigms are but culturally different versions of the same ontological affirmation.

Conclusion: The Reality of Hope

From the wisdom of the past we learn that "hope that is seen is not hope." Relationally rephrased, it is the insight that hope is not the reality of "the Future," since the latter has no reality. Rather, hope is the reality of futurity; it is present anticipation. Today one hears a great deal about global planning, but from a relational perspective the caveat comes that *planning* is not the actualization of "the Future"; it is rather only the reality of planning. Planning is not thereby discouraged; what is discouraged is the *allzumenschlich* proclivity for ontologizing what *is* not present.

While the analytic of hope advanced in this essay has the potential for relieving some of the anxiety associated with illusory notions of time and reality, the relational metaphysical schema which informs this analytic has the power to speak materially of the content of world hope. That "the Future" is uncertain follows not from some human weakness but from the abstract nature of "the Future." The emptiness of "the Future" is compensated for in experience by the fullness of futurity, that is, of hope. To the degree that cultural despair is a function of inadequate conceptions of reality, the positive value of improved conceptions should be apparent. Since relational metaphysics does not subscribe to the ontologies of either Idealism or Realism, it undermines the extremes of subjectivism and objectivism which account for much of the cultural disorder of our times. Personal and social wholeness, desperately sought by so many in fragmented ways, must receive universal priority; but not simply as an ideal, for ideas have only ideality. A goal has only the reality of the means, hence the proverbial wisdom about means and ends. Let me illustrate this wisdom.

During the late 1960s a friend sent me a greeting card, on the face of which was printed:

> Peace is not the goal,
> Peace is the way.

By analogy it may be said: Hope is the actual form of the Not Yet, the only actuality it has. Therefore, hope is the generic form in which the goal of the human future becomes the way.

7 | The "Historical Past" as Reified Memory: toward a Hermeneutics of Immediacy as Applied to Texts and Ritual

There is no notion of experience more stubborn and persistent than that of "the Past." The preferred ambulatory directivity of the human body and the virtually absolute directivity of human vision conspire to dictate a protometaphysics of "the Past" as a domain once for all travelled and no longer "in view." There is even a presentiment of this protometaphysics in Heraclitus's notion of "the same river." The formative power of this protometaphysics of "the Past" over later sophisticated Western metaphysical thinking led German philosophers to identify the whatness of things by the term *das Wesen*—a notion correctly indicated by the philosopher Ernst Bloch as derivative of the verbal expression *das Gewesene*—"what has been." Cartesian analytic geometry, which served as the coordinate reference frame of Newtonian physics, dignified the naive metaphysical notion of the asymmetrical directivity of time, even though dynamic reversibility was said to hold for any physical system. The primitive sense of qualitative temporality in Christian eschatology was early altered into a linear quantitative temporal asymmetry, and the biblical narrative conceived as a unity came to be interpreted through the speculative device of a linearly temporal "history of salvation."

These cultural phenomena which manifest a tendency to absolutize commonsense notions of time serve to illustrate a human proclivity for reifying temporal features of experience. It will be the purpose of this paper to raise questions about the metaphysical warrant for this practice in view of the claim to be set forth that temporal features of experience yield abstractions only, not fundamentals. And in view of the specific topic of this paper it shall be my aim to assess the adequacy of ontological claims about "the Past." This essay is to be interpreted as a logical extension of the "phenomenology of temporality" developed in an earlier article which sought to establish the inappropriateness of ontological claims about "the Future."[1]

In developing the argument about the metaphysical status of "the Past" I shall be governed by immediate hermeneutical goals. Four antitheses will be examined:

- "The Historical Past" as Transcendent Object
  versus The Immediacy of "Pastness"
- Narrative Texts as Historical Records
  versus Narrative Texts as Codified Memory
- Method as Mediation
  versus The Hermeneutics of Immediacy
- Ritual as Mediated Re-Enactment of "The Past"
  versus Ritual as Enacted Immediacy

My *modus operandi* will be to argue for the conceptual superiority of the latter thesis in each case by indicating that the former is based directly or inferentially upon a reified abstraction.

---

[1]Cf. essay 6, above.

"The Historical Past" as Transcendent Object
versus the Immediacy of "Pastness"

In the relational theory which I have set forth in recent articles[2] it is claimed that *relations* are fundamental, and that all *relata*, such as subject-selves, object-selves, phenomenal things, even mind and brain, are derivative notions, that is to say, abstractions. I have further indicated the extent to which this claim is commensurate with the notion of Pure Experience according to which Immediacy is all there is. Perhaps I should review these claims briefly, since the hermeneutics of Immediacy to be developed in this paper is grounded upon them.

The theory assumes that experience is all there is, and that experience is always "Pure"; it is exhaustively Immediacy, or in a co-ordinate idiom, Relat*ing*. In Immediacy there is no subject, no object, no prior, and no posterior; for Immediacy is a unity. Distinctions of subject and object, and of space and time, arise only through reflection upon Immediacy, that is, through mediation. Reflection is but one type of activity, one type of Immediacy. The process of mediation cannot be trusted to yield reliable information about "what is" (Immediacy), because what it analyzes into parts *is not* (= is not Immediate), even though the act of reflection is itself immediate. Immediacy is experienc*ing*; it is not the product of an experienc*er*, since the latter is a derivative of experienc*ing*. Otherwise the anomaly arises that the experienc*er* precedes experienc*ing*, which would be empirical nonsense; for there can be no *prior* within a unitive act, nor can there be constituent parts. Further, time and space are but derivatives of certain textural features of Immediacy; accordingly, experience is not "located in space and time." Relevant to this claim is the judgment, commensurate with good physics and metaphysics, that space and time represent not fundamental things, but simply "languages" of measurement. They emerge through extension of the aforementioned textural features of experience and are useful

---

[2]Cf. essays 1 and 3, above.

abstractions for "the middle range of the empirical," but dissolve into theoretical vagueness at both ends of this empirical spectrum. Although "time" is not fundamental, there is about experience a dimension of "temporality" which is not to be denied. Two modes of this temporality are of special interest to us: "futurity" and "pastness." From a phenomenological point of view, "futurity" is the name we give to the anticipatory mode of Immediacy; "pastness," to the memoriter mode of Immediacy. When and if reified, "futurity" gives rise to the notion of "the Future"; similarly, "pastness," when and if reified, translates into "the Past." From the perspective of relational metaphysics and Immediacy, "pastness" and "futurity" are experientially available, whereas their respective reifications, "the Past" and "the Future," represent abstractions raised to the level of fundamentals. Specifically, the reification of "the pastness of Immediacy" into "the Past" transcendentalizes it into an object no longer available experientially. The "pastness" that is given in the memoriter mode of Immediacy is fully present. The metaphysical interpretation of this "pastness" as a "record(-ing)" of something absent (= not available), namely, "the historical Past," transforms "pastness" into an elusive object of search; as non-Immediate it must be mediated by method in a process which is universally conceded to be asymptotic.

From the relational perspective the metaphysics of "the historical Past" must be judged to be guilty of "the fallacy of misplaced concreteness," for it ontologizes an abstraction. Although many domains of human experience have been adversely affected by this spurious ontology, I have chosen to focus on the one which has perhaps most deeply and adversely affected Judeo-Christianity, namely, hermeneutical theory. Specifically I shall deal with the hermeneutics of narrative texts of eminent religious literature which has suffered most at the hands of modern interpreters.

Narrative Texts as Historical "Records" versus Narrative Texts as Codified Memory

Historical-critical scholarship came of age in the eighteenth and nineteenth centuries through the instrumentality of reason, that is, through the appeal to judgment as the final arbiter of the meaning of texts. One immediate result of rationalistic hermeneutics was the instrumentalizing of texts of eminent literature by addressing to them modern questions forged from rationalistic priorities. In place of the earlier function of such texts whereby they stood as the symbolic presencing of reality, a hermeneutics of suspicion was devised which treated these texts as "signs," that is, as representations of what is absent, namely, the "real" events behind the texts. The basic assumption of historical scholarship applied to narrative texts for almost two centuries has been that they are to be evaluated primarily as *records*; the most visible result of this practice was that progress in such scholarship was measured by the criterion of success in operationalizing one basic question: is the particular narrative text under review a reliable historical *record* of those events it *purports* to report?

According to the hermeneutics of Immediacy narrative texts of eminent literature are to be evaluated exhaustively in accord with their intentionality as derived solely from their "narrativity." I intentionally isolate their "intentionality" rather than the supposed intentionality of their separate authors, since it follows from the hermeneutics of Immediacy that all talk of "the mind of the author" shifts the hermeneutical enterprise away from the text (and thus what is at hand) toward an object of search to be mediated by method. I have developed the intentionality of mythical narratives elsewhere[3] and cannot use this occasion to reestablish that line of argument, except to say that my conclusion is that mythical narratives intend to *image* reality as relatedness. Hermeneutics becomes the unfolding of this intentionality *sensu stricto*.

The antithesis advanced under section 1 can serve to broaden the base of the claims I am making about mythic texts and their appropriate interpretation.

---

[3]Cf. essays 2 and 4, above.

The view that narrative texts of eminent literature represent "records" is bound up with the assumption that they "take us back" to what is no longer immediate, namely, "the Past"—the "historical Past," if you will. They are thus "signs" of what is absent, and are accordingly to be evaluated primarily in terms of their adequacy for determining and authenticating "what actually happened." Conversely, in accord with the hermeneutics of Immediacy, such texts re-*présent* features of Immediacy whose narrative form justifies calling them codifications of "pastness." It follows that they are present forms of fixed memory which re-*présent* what is present: the prefix *re* is justified with respect to their narrative form, while the special sense of the verb "to make present" is justified in view of Gadamer's notion of "presencing." The net effect of this argument is that narratives are "symbols" rather than signs, in that they announce what is at hand rather than *sign*-aling what is absent (note: "absent" by virtue of a metaphysics of "the Past").

I am tempted to substantiate this view of narrative hermeneutics by recourse to the excellent book by Hans Frei, *The Eclipse of Biblical Narrative*,[4] which came to my attention quite recently. Rather than doing so, I shall present a very generalized picture of the matrix out of which emerged the metaphysics of "the historical Past" and its attendant hermeneutics. Prior to the rise of Rationalism, *mythos* (μῦθος) and *logos* (λόγος) were co-aspectual terms for the "stories of the gods." With the coming of Rationalism, *logos* became *ratio*, and *mythos* became *pseudos* (ψεῦδος). In fact it can be argued that *logos* became *ratio* by reducing *mythos* to *pseudos*. Thus *mythos* in the modern sense (for example, in Bultmann's demythologizing program to the extent that it negated cosmological aspects of myth) was the creation of *ratio*, effected through a ruthless negation. Those who continued in their religious traditions despite the onslaught of Rationalism took on the character of their opposition to

---

[4]Hans Frei, *The Eclipse of Biblical Narrative: A Study of Eighteenth and Nineteenth Century Hermeneutics* (New Haven: Yale University Press, 1980).

naturalism, that is, they became super-*naturalists* through a negation of a negation: *mythos* is *not* a *pseudos*.

The rationalistic negation of *mythos* took the positive form of a "quest" for historical truth, that is, for "what actually happened" *behind* the tenuous records. The supernaturalists defended the historical veracity of the narratives. The hidden assumption within both positions was that narratives are *records*, that is, that their intentionality was to provide access to "the Past." This assumption represented something truly new, a modern novelty resulting from the rationalists' erroneous judgment that narrative texts of religious traditions were intentionally *referential*. While the rationalists simply denied the referents as mythically portrayed, the supernaturalists, in affirming the reality of those referents—in this case historical events—were seduced into the rationalists' theory of mythical discourse. In pre-rationalistic mythic awareness, the differentiation of "historical truth versus falsity" was not fundamental; this distinction had not yet become the defining characteristic of belief, as it did with the advent of Rationalism. I shall return to this issue in the third section where I shall seek to reassess the role of David Friedrich Strauss by means of this perspective.

The rationalists' assumption of the historical intentionality of narrative texts of eminent religious literature deeply affected the shape of things to come, especially in biblical scholarship. From the time of Lorenzo Valla's exposure of the Donation of Constantine, the power of historical-critical method was turned ruthlessly upon all documents purporting to offer historical foundations for religious beliefs. No question was more paramount in biblical scholarship than that of "genuineness," and documents that failed this test suffered untold neglect. One has only to recall the second-class citizenship of the Gospel of John and the Book of Acts in the second half of the nineteenth century to be reminded of the power of the new methods. The terms "genuineness" and "historical" entered into a holy alliance at the hands of the Rationalists who were convinced of their synonymity. Let me be clear: I am not arguing that the hermeneutics of Immediacy calls for a reassertion of the historical veracity of these documents. Rather I want to make the point that the intentionality of biblical narratives must not be sought by operationalizing the concept of record. Since the rationalists instrumentalized many of these texts for the purpose of establishing what lay *behind* them, I should even question whether it is appropriate to speak of their efforts as truly hermeneutical. A subtle but fundamental shift had occurred: explication of the texts had been replaced by reconstruction of the "historical Past."

Another consequence for later biblical scholarship of the rationalists' assumptions about narrative was the ensuing preoccupation with *history*. The new coinage included phrases like "the historical Jesus," *Heilsgeschichte*, the history of Israel, God who acts in history, and "faith and history." The notion of "history" seemed ready-made to fill the lacuna created by Protestantism's neglect of nature; it was easily convertible into existential language, and—like the medieval concept of nature, it too was a religious term, although in both instances they did not appear to be so at the time. Perhaps I should elaborate upon this latter claim: a perusal of most of the instances of the term "historical" in modern theological literature should convince one that theologians have understood it against the background of a two-dimensional cosmology, namely, the human sphere as demarcated from and by the sphere of the divine. The rise of modern biblical theology coincided with the invention of this cosmology, and its decline coincided with the realization that it was a religious contrivance. Probably this is what James Barr means when he argues that the characteristic coinages of biblical theologians developed straight out of "pulpit rhetoric."[5] While I am convinced that Barr has not sufficiently purged his own thinking of the rhetoric as it pertains to the term "historical," I am particularly indebted to him for his insight that the concept of *Heilsgeschichte* developed out of the extension of the notion of historical intentionality

---

[5]James Barr, "Story and History in Biblical Theology," *Journal of Religion* 56 (1976): 3.

of single texts to the entire narrative sequence of the Old and New Testaments conceived as a unity, that is, as "a single story."

It is even possible to understand the import of and necessity for Lessing's famous question—"How can accidental facts of history become the basis for the eternal truths of reason?"—as an emergent from Rationalism's fixation on the "historical" intentionality of the biblical texts. The formative power of this polarity in Hegel and Kierkegaard rests on the cultural currency of this rationalistic distinction; and while I should be the last to trivialize the monumental edifices which each in his own way raised on his foundation, I should like to suggest that the realization of this common assumption might go a long way toward accounting for the specific "architecture" of these edifices.

Before leaving this issue of the impact of rationalistic historicism upon hermeneutics I should like to make one final point. It is that even the modern development of *allgemeine Hermeneutik* out of the earlier specialized hermeneutics of texts has in part taken the form of a major debate—between Gadamer and Ricoeur on the one hand, and Betti and Hirsch on the other—specifically over the issue of "hermeneutics and historicism."[6] It is certainly the case that General Hermeneutics is an attempt to move beyond "explication of texts" to the unfolding of the nature of understanding as such; nevertheless, the "historical" issue has dominated General Hermeneutics since the middle of the nineteenth century, as is evident from the contributions of Dilthey, Collingwood, and Wach. It is the singular genius of Gadamer to have redirected the hermeneutical task and to have reconceived it in a form which is compatible with recent exploratory reconsiderations of the intentionality of narrative as story. Ricoeur, who owes as much to Gadamer as does Gadamer to Heidegger, seems to me not to have freed himself from the bias toward the referential character of myth whose origins and fateful consequences I have tried to articulate above.

---

[6]Cf. Hans-Georg Gadamer, *Truth and Method* (New York: The Seabury Press, 1975) esp. Supplement I, "Hermeneutics and Historicism," 460-91.

Having said this much, I should now like to move into the discussion of the third antithesis, noting in advance that my preference for the latter "term" owes something to Gadamer's classic, *Truth and Method*. Nevertheless, the reasons for my recourse to Gadamer's idiom lie in my own metaphysical work, as should be evident in what follows.

Method as Mediation
versus the Hermeneutics of Immediacy

Historical-critical scholarship has been committed to the principle that the success of efforts to understand texts is a singular function of the invention of adequate methodologies. It has relentlessly patrolled its own border to keep out those who claim to have immediate, nonmethodological access to the meaning of texts. This defensive posture seemed fully justified in view of the fact that historical-critical scholarship emerged precisely for the purpose of negating previous uncritical dogmas of privileged truth. The methodologies which have been generated out of historical-critical inquiry are products of enormous ingenuity motivated by intensive passion for naked truth. What Schweitzer called "the making and testing of hypotheses" has been the distinctive *modus operandi* of critical scholarship which determined to model itself on the supposedly objective methods used in the natural sciences, and thereby to match the great success of the latter in countering speculative dogmas of the world.

Admittedly, toward the end of the nineteenth century biblical theologians did begin to cite certain limits of historical-critical method as a way of opening the hermeneutic enterprise to aspects of the texts which proved to be closed to scientific methods per se; nevertheless, these theologians in the main did not oppose those methods. Rather they respected critical method within imposed limits, being fully aware that it was precisely the unconditional commitment to method that had led to the discovery of its limits with respect to the character of the text.

To the extent that the recently emerging methodologies use *story* and *narrative* as primary paradigms, they constitute a major departure from earlier historicism. In addition to supporting these more economical hermeneutical ventures, the hermeneutics of Immediacy goes beyond them in locating the metaphysical problematic of earlier theories in their uncritical notion of reference, and in setting forth a general hermeneutics of experience within which the notion of "the historical Past" is deprived of its supposed fundamentality.

According to the hermeneutics of Immediacy, method must be judged to be an act of *mediation*, a reflective process characterized by the representation of what is (no longer) present, hence what is not immediate. It is an attempt to recapture by reconstruction what is in "the Past." This approach overlooks the Immediacy of narrative; for the text *stands before* us (= is Immediate) in the form of codified memory. In recognition of this fact it is the singular task of hermeneutics to take account of what is at hand rather than to negate what is Immediate by instrumentalizing the text for the dubious purpose of *mediating* what is absent (not available).

The hermeneutics of suspicion with its prime category of "search" for a mediated surrogate for what is Immediate (that is, the text) was based on metaphysical assumptions of insufficient generality. One has but to consider ancient and Eastern traditions of knowledge to realize the extent to which *method* in the West was conceived as *techné*, which Heidegger rightly characterized as manipulative and calculative thinking in which the *known* becomes an object external to the *knower*. Knowledge was no longer a revelation of soteriological power, but an object empowered by the knower. That contrast is present in the thought of the Apostle Paul when he distinguished between "knowing in part" and "knowing as we are fully known." The loss of the distinction in the West resulted in a Western antagonism toward myth, an antagonism which never existed in the East. I am convinced that the present growing hostility toward method is consciously and unconsciously informed by a renewed awareness of this long-neglected broader and deeper *gnosis*.

As a way of demonstrating the cogency of the hermeneutics of Immediacy over one of "search," I should like to advert to a major nineteenth-century theologian who has since been championed as a leading representative of the "search" mentality, but whose thought needs to be reassessed in view of the hermeneutical perspective I have set forth above. The theologian in question is David Friedrich Strauss, that herald of modernity who—like all the prophets—was "without honor in his own country."

It has been customary, at least since the time Schweitzer introduced the concept of "the quest of the historical Jesus," to describe a variety of disjunctive studies in the nineteenth century, to regard Strauss's *magnum opus* as the classic piece of "quest" literature. Instead of giving the full title of Strauss's first edition, namely, *Das Leben Jesu kritisch bearbeitet,* Schweitzer listed it in the abbreviated form, *Das Leben Jesu,* and thus fostered his own notion that Strauss's first edition intended to be a "life of Jesus." With that self-made advantage Schweitzer could easily justify his lament that it is difficult "if not, strictly speaking, impossible . . . to discover what he really thinks is moving behind [*sic*] the curtain of myth."[7] Others have since bemoaned the extreme paucity of Strauss's conclusions about "what really happened," and have accordingly called his effort negative and inconclusive. Van Harvey, for example, recently published the judgment that Strauss was a "failure" in that he "failed to discern the question to which the New Testament documents were intended as an answer," so that "the positive meaning of the text, as Schweitzer observes, escapes him."[8] More recently, the late Norman Perrin stated that the task to which Strauss set himself in the early 1830s was that of "writing a critical life of Christ."[9] In his crit-

---

[7]Albert Schweitzer, *The Quest of the Historical Jesus: A Critical Study of its Progress from Reimarus to Wrede* (New York: Macmillan Company, 1950 ed.) 90.

[8]Van A. Harvey, "D. F. Strauss' *Life of Jesus* Revisited," *Church History* 30 (1961): 205.

[9]Norman Perrin, *Rediscovering the Teachings of Jesus* (New York: Harper and Row, 1967) 211.

ical introduction to the new edition of Strauss's *Life of Jesus Criti-cally Examined*, Peter Hodgson seemed to waver between a classical Schweitzerian position and one which rightfully breaks free from it. For, while he incisively notes that "Strauss was uninter-ested in providing a synthetic portrayal of the life of Jesus" and that "such a disinterest made his work appear more historically sceptical than it really was,"[10] Hodgson goes on to reflect the usual notion of Strauss as a "failure":

> With the concept of myth, Strauss uses a *positive* criterion to achieve *negative* results. Whereas the historian is ordinarily interested in defining critically what is historical, *Strauss has no criterion for isolating authentic historical materials.* It is by no means necessarily the case that, where the mythical criterion fails to apply, historical traditions are present.[11]

While Hodgson wants to conclude from this remark that Strauss is no "ordinary" historian, I should like to suggest that Strauss will al-ways remain an enigma if we continue to assume that his intention—in 1835—was primarily historical. In my opinion it is only from the perspective of the misconception of Strauss's intention (in 1835) that it can be argued—with Harvey—that "Strauss regards myth as a historical-critical device especially useful to reconstruction be-cause it enables the historian to separate fact from fiction."[12] If I can demonstrate that Strauss's intention was not primarily historical, the judgment that Strauss, measured by his own intention in 1835, was a failure, would collapse.

It is my belief that Strauss was an eminent success in what he set out to achieve, namely, to determine the *character* of the text of the Gospels. His judgment that they represent mythical discourse was a provocative alternative to previous theories; it was only when

---

[10]David Friedrich Strauss, *The Life of Jesus Critically Examined*, ed. by Peter C. Hodgson, trans. George Eliot, The Life of Jesus Series, ed. Leander E. Keck (Philadelphia: Fortress Press, 1972) xxxi.

[11]Ibid., xxvii.

[12]Harvey, "D. F. Strauss' *Life of Jesus* Revisted," 205.

he was under fire from his critics that he altered his work in subsequent editions whose format suggested to later interpreters that
Strauss was dominated by a "quest" mentality. If what I have stated
above is trustworthy, it strongly supports the novel idea that
Strauss may have been the last great biblical scholar of the nineteenth century to focus on the text rather than to instrumentalize it
for the purpose of historical reconstruction.

I should like to advance three arguments in support of the thesis
about Strauss just proposed. The first argument is that Strauss's
stated intention in the edition of 1835 was not to "reconstruct the
life of Jesus," but—in his own words—to determine "whether in fact
and to what extent the ground on which we stand in the Gospels is
historical."[13] I interpret these words as announcing an inquiry into
textuality rather than historicity, although earlier interpreters of
Strauss imposed the latter meaning on his words. A subsequent remark of Strauss seems to me to reinforce the claim that his focus
is on the nature of the text:

> To investigate the internal grounds of credibility in relation to each de-
> tail given in the gospels (for it is with them alone we are here concerned)
> and to test the probability or improbability of their being the production of
> eyewitnesses, or of competently informed writers, is the sole [*sic*] object
> of the present work. [14]

---

[13]Strauss, *Life of Jesus*, li.

[14]Ibid., 70. A citation of the larger context will strengthen the claim I wish to
make:

> The exegesis of the ancient church set out from the double presup-
> position: first, that the Gospels contained a history, and secondly, that this
> history was a supernatural one. Rationalism rejected the latter of these
> presuppositions, but only to cling more tenaciously to the former, main-
> taining that these books present unadulterated, though only natural, his-
> tory. Science cannot rest satisfied with this half-measure: the other
> presupposition also must be relinquished, and the inquiry must first be
> made whether in fact, and to what extent, the ground on which we stand
> in the Gospels is historical.

Athough there is much material in the 1400-page work that could be interpreted as reflecting historicist priorities, I am fully convinced that the claim that Strauss was a historian (in 1835) is a judgment that reflects the priorities of his subsequent interpreters rather than his own at that time.

A second argument in favor of the interpretation of Strauss as a hermeneuticist rather than a historicist is the support given to it by Karl Barth who quoted Strauss to this effect: "I am not a historian; with me everything has proceeded from dogmatic (or rather anti-dogmatic) concerns."[15] It is remarkable that Barth is virtually alone in deciphering, albeit incompletely, what I have stated to be Strauss's true intention in 1835. One paragraph from Barth is especially illuminating:

> Strauss not only does not discover a "historical core" to the life of Jesus, but does not even begin to enquire after it. He does not deny a historical core as a possibility, as Bruno Bauer did later, and as Kalthoff and Artur Drews have done in our century. But neither does he assert and demonstrate a historical core to the life of Jesus. Strauss is not interested in it. His work is purely critical. He is only concerned with showing the presence and origin of myth, whatever might be "behind" it.[16]

It is a further confirmation of the main thesis advanced above that Barth finds it strange that by 1864 Strauss did in fact venture a quest for such a historical core of the life of Jesus.[17]

It is commonly assumed by modern interpreters of Strauss that he simply believed the admixture of myth in the Gospel stories to be more substantial than that claimed by his rationalist opponents. If that be true, then I fail to see how he achieved his primary goal of transcending the supernaturalist-rationalist dilemma. My consid-

---

[15]David Friedrich Strauss, Letter of 22 July 1846; cited from Karl Barth, *Protestant Thought: From Rousseau to Ritschl* (New York: Harper & Brothers, 1959) 346.

[16]Ibid., 381.

[17]Ibid., 385.

ered judgment is that Strauss did in fact move beyond this dilemma by questioning the assumption shared by both the supernaturalists and rationalists, namely, *that the texts intended to be records* at all. Strauss discovered precisely what he set out to find, namely, the character of the text. He was an exemplar of hermeneutical method rather than of historicism. I submit that the inability of most of Strauss's modern interpreters to resolve the paradoxes of his career rests upon their failure to understand what he set out to accomplish.

My third argument is of a different order: it is that to the extent that it is proper to determine Strauss's intention from his published writings, it is unwise to define his intention as primarily historical. Seldom in the two volume work does he even broach the historical question, a fact that troubles his historicist interpreters. Schweitzer's frustration before this fact is worth repeating:

> There are . . . a number of incidental remarks which contain the suggestion of a positive construction of the life of Jesus. If they were taken out of their contexts and brought together they would yield a picture which would have points of contact with the latest eschatological view. Strauss, however, deliberately restricts his positive suggestions to these few detached remarks. He follows no line to its conclusion. Each separate problem is indeed considered, and light is thrown upon it from various quarters with much critical skill. But he will not venture on a solution of any of them. Sometimes, when he thinks he has gone too far in the way of positive suggestion, he deliberately wipes it all out again with some expression of scepticism.[18]

The simplest resolution of Schweitzer's dilemma is to locate it within his own historicist agenda; Strauss makes perfect sense once the historicist intention is left out of regard.

It may be asked why I have devoted so much attention in so brief a paper on hermeneutics to what may appear to be a digression. In view of the importance of Strauss to both theologians and philosophers it seemed to me that a reversal of judgment about his inten-

---

[18]Schweitzer, *The Quest*, 90.

tion would allow me to claim him as an ally in the proposed hermeneutics of Immediacy. My conclusion is that Strauss's intention was hermeneutical rather than historical, and that judged hermeneutically Strauss was a success. Further, the purity of his effort to discover the intentionality of the text gives his work a new relevance for the modern hermeneutical renaissance which affirms the priority of textuality over historicity.

Ritual as Re-enactment of "The Past" versus Ritual as Enacted Immediacy

Just as there is a revival of interest in hermeneutics, so there is a new sense of the role of ritual in social life. Accordingly, I should like to suggest ways in which the hermeneutics of Immediacy might serve to enrich the current exploration of the intentionality of ritual, ancient and modern.

In the Western context of historicist metaphysics ritual came to be regarded as re-enactment of "the Past." It was largely interpreted as the "hold of 'the Past' " upon subsequent generations of devotees. By ritual re-enactment the tradition was re-lived, that is, quickened again. Modern secularism spurned precisely this irrelevance of ancient traditions too long determinative of human life. Rationalistically regarded, rituals were interpreted as signs, that is, as "announcements of what is absent." Through ritual re-enactment there could be mediated to the participant *une realite passé*, an absent God, or a *deus absconditus*. In all such instances the "reality" celebrated was historic and/or transcendent, and hence not Immediate.

From the perspective of a hermeneutics of Immediacy ritual regains its truly symbolic power, which is to announce the presence of what is present (Gadamer). Thus with respect to its ontological depth, ritual represents not "what is absent," but what is truly present—a dimension which is captured by the term "enactment" rather than "re-enactment." But since not all acts are ritual in character, a clue to what is distinctive about ritual lies in its relation to memory.

Ritual is linked to the memoriter mode of experience, a fact which accounts for the human proclivity for interpreting it as re-enactment. I prefer to think of ritual as *enacted memory*; for just as it is ontologically true to say that a ritual act is not a re-enactment of what happened in "the Past," so it is derivately true to say that what is happening in it "presents itself" as "happening again." The word "again" is justified in view of the ontology of Immediacy which recognizes the experiential feature of "pastness."

Ritual is also related to the anticipatory mode of Immediacy. The acts are staged "with a view to" certain benefits, however conceptualized. The notion of "messianic banquets" which anticipate "the Messianic Banquet" is evidence that certain ritual acts are linked to the anticipatory mode. Although it is beyond the scope of this essay further to explore the notion of "futurity" and of its derivative, "the Future,"[19] it must be enjoined that the hermeneutics of Immediacy places severe restraints upon any effort to probe the ontology of ritual-as-anticipation.

---

[19]Cf. essay 6, above.

8 | Interpretation: Art or Science?

Interpretation is usually represented as a science, that is, as an activity to be performed after the mastery of the appropriate methods and tools of scholarship. This claim is the very foundation of critical scholarship whose professional guilds are comprised of those uniquely certified to speak expertly about the meaning of things, whether these things be texts or phenomena. The *myth* of science (scholarship, *Wissenschaft*) is the direct correlation between "method and truth"; the *dynamic* of science is the perfecting of method; the *goal* of science is—as its name indicates—"knowledge." Its eminent success in the modern world rests on its proven excellence when compared with some of the best guesses of precritical cultures. The growth of critical inquiry in the West resulted inevitably in a denigration of mythical modes of thought; I say *inevitably*, because critical inquiry has its origins in Rationalism's relentless attack upon mythical, precritical thinking. To appeal to a famous Socratic injunction: the "unexamined" became the "worthless"—"examination" here being taken to mean "analysis" and "demonstration." "Thinking" became synonymous with "reflection," and "insight" with "intelligibility."

No aspect of experience has escaped the rigorous scrutiny of Reason in search of truth; no precritical conclusion about experience and its features has been immune from criticism. Modernity is by and large defined by passionate commitment to rational goals and criteria. Whatever has survived from precritical times as a living force today has had to prove itself before the court of reason, and maintains itself today in competition with cultural forms generated directly from modern Rationalism. I am referring especially to the residual role of religion in modern scientific culture. Ingenious theories have been devised to insure the conviviality of religion and science. Here I am speaking of "science" in the modern popular sense of "natural science," but only momentarily, for I want to return to the notion of science as "critical inquiry," and to indicate the deep impact such inquiry has had upon religious understanding.

Scholarship is no stranger to religious faith, for one of the most impressive strands of Western culture has been the search for an understanding commensurate with faith. In the Enlightenment, however, scholarship was redefined as "historical-critical research" and one of its most distinctive tasks was the application of critical methodology to the settlement of questions of truth, whether of the truth-claims of revelation or of popular wisdom. Since Western culture had previously been uniquely shaped by commitments to scripture and Church tradition, it was inevitable that some of its best minds would test these foundations by recourse to the new standards of worth.

Modern critical biblical scholarship was generated out of the matrix of Rationalism and has been characterized by high standards of professional excellence that have insured its academic respectability and viability in the community of scholars representing all modern disciplines. This is as it should be, and the continuing challenge of biblical scholarship is to maintain its scholarly excellence while ever seeking to do justice to its unique task. Biblical scholars have enjoyed high visibility both among those engaged in building the foundations of Modernity and among those who have begun to subject those foundations to severe testing. This last remark, however, runs a little ahead of the scenario of Modernity I am presenting and should be held in abeyance. This move will allow us to return to our brief consideration of the origins and commitments of modern biblical criticism.

Prior to the Age of Reason biblical scholarship was—with a few notable exceptions—an activity of persons functioning "within faith," that is, of persons who—however divided over matters of faith—viewed themselves as somehow operating under the authority of scripture. In the Enlightenment a new "breed" of scholars arose—persons who questioned the very authority of scripture itself in the interest of what was then called "free thinking." The new "sanctity" was the sanctity of pure thought before which nothing was "sacred" that laid claim to truth on other grounds. A mitigating factor which somehow redeemed the whole enterprise was the tenacious hold which Pietism exerted on the minds of many of its principal figures. For such Pietism insured that the attention of some of the best minds would be directed toward scriptural study at a time when there were ever more alluring pursuits.

The new bibilical criticism was so revolutionary and liberating that all previous efforts to "interpret" scripture were judged inadequate, and were often held up to ridicule. Only the biblical scholarship of the Reformers maintained respectability in the face of this more radical reformation—that of thought itself. This respect was due to the obvious fact that the Protestant Reformation was a kind of proto-critical phenomenon foreshadowing the arrival of the Age of Reason. This state of affairs is evident in one of the most ambitious of modern attempts to trace the course of modern New Testament scholarship namely, Kümmel's *The New Testament: A History of the Investigation of its Problems*[1]. That it highlights critical

---

[1] Werner Georg Kümmel, *The New Testament: A History of the Investigation of its Problems*, trans. S. McLean Gilmour and Howard C. Kee (Nashville: Abingdon Press, 1972).

scholarship is apparent from its format, for Kümmel devotes only 27
of its 406 pages to the so-called "precritical period" which, for him
includes—in the specially qualified way indicated above—the "Period of the Reformation." His defense of his decision to neglect pre-
Enlightenment New Testament scholarship is instructive for our
purposes:

> It is impossible to speak of a scientific view of the New Testament until
> the New Testament became the object of investigation as an independent
> body of literature with historical interest, as a collection of writings that
> could be considered apart from the Old Testament and without dogmatic
> or creedal bias. Since such a view began to prevail only during the course
> of the eighteenth century, earlier discussion of the New Testament can
> only be referred to as the prehistory of New Testament scholarship.

He continues;

> It is true, of course, that the writings of the New Testament were ex-
> pounded in countless commentaries from the time of the earliest church
> fathers and that thereby much historical knowledge and also many a rel-
> evant insight were handed on or discovered. But even where a special ef-
> fort was made in such exposition to be true to the literal [*sic*] sense of the
> text, as, for example, by the School of Antioch . . . such exegesis was not
> undertaken with any conscious historical purpose, and was also pre-
> served only within the framework of ecclesiastical tradition. Conse-
> quently, it is improper to speak of scientific study of the New Testament
> or a historical approach to primitive Christianity prior to the
> Enlightenment.[2]

The equating of "scientific" and "historical" in this quotation is quite
revealing, and I shall return to this issue shortly. The heart of Kümmel's book is a survey of the beginnings of the scientific investigation of the New Testament, and of its development as a "rigorously
historical discipline." Towards the end of the volume he gives serious attention to the "theological emphasis" that developed in biblical
scholarship after World War I as a corrective to the excessive prom-
ises and claims of "historical-critical" inquiry as applied to the New

---

[2]Ibid., 13.

Testament. Any person knowledgeable in this field is aware that in the twentieth century "historical" and "theological" priorities in biblical scholarship have coexisted in some tension, since no equation of their relationship has met with success. Leading biblical scholars who advocated "theological method" did not abandon historical criticism, since they knew that the former had emerged at the experienced limits of the latter. Since it became canonical to think that "theological" awareness could only so emerge, there was no inclination to repudiate the positive gains of critical thinking over pre-critical—even though the latter was somehow more resonant with "theological" exegesis than with "historical" inquiry. For, after all, the "theological" message was available in texts of the past, many of them narrative in nature, and thus apparently "historical" in intention.

Rationalism's unique legacy to textual inquiry was the claim that because narrative texts intend to represent the past, the primary task of the critic of narrative texts of eminent literature is to determine their historical worth. The desire to have the past "as it really was" led scholars to instrumentalize extant ancient texts as a means of "reconstructing" the past. The text became the *means* to the truth *behind* the texts. It happened in biblical scholarship as elsewhere that the texts which fared best under this scrutiny were held in highest regard, and conversely, that texts which fared poorly were largely neglected. Special instances of this reduction of narrative texts to secondary status were the Fourth Gospel (when judged within the context of the "Quest of the Historical Jesus") and the Book of Acts (when bought under scrutiny by the Tübingen School within the context of its effort to establish the true history of the Apostolic Age).

The net effect of such critical devaluation of biblical documents was that the earlier conception of the *truth-in-and-of-the-text* was transfigured into a later notion, rationalistic in origin, of the *truth-about-the-text*. The distinction between the *truth-in-and-of-the-text* and the *truth-about-the-text* I have often delineated by recourse to

Gadamer's distinction between sign and symbol.[3] A sign *sign*-als what is absent; it re-*présents* what is no longer at hand. On the contrary a symbol announces the presence of what *is* present. The notion of the truth-*about*-the-text—which results in the correlative notion of the truth-*behind*-the-text is tantamount to regarding the text as a "sign," as a re-*présent*-ation of what is absent, namely, the past events "recorded" in it. The precritical assumption of the truth *in-and-of-the-text* accepts the text as symbol, as a re-*présent*-ing of what is present. In the latter, the task of interpretation is conceived as a "letting be" of what "is" rather than as a re-accessing of what "was," but is no longer! It advocates a "listening" to the text, whereas critical method reduces the text to an objective instrument of discovery, an *organon*. Rational method becomes a relentless "search" for truth, a quest which on its own admission is necessarily asymptotic. For the high regard in which historical-critical and scientific theories are held is a measure of the degree, not of their finality, but of their *probability*.

The two approaches to the task of interpretation raise fundamental questions:

- What is the intentionality of narrative texts of eminent literature?
- When can such texts be said to be understood?
- What is the nature of understanding?
- What is the proper role of the interpreter?
- How are the assumptions and conclusions of the interpreter to be evaluated?

The urgency of these questions and the difficulties which have arisen with respect to the answers offered by historical-critical methodology have combined to generate a science of interpretation, that is, a theory of theory, a meta-theory of interpretation. I can but briefly indicate some of its major developments.

---

[3]Hans-Georg Gadamer, *Truth and Method* (New York: The Seabury Press, 1975).

Under the influence of the Reformers, Schleiermacher sought to set interpretation on a solid footing by arguing that a text is understood when one determines "what the author meant." This quest for the "mind of the author" seemed to restore objectivity to interpretation which had long been plagued with such subjective notions as "what God meant" in scripture. The history of interpretation indicated to Schleiermacher that the text had lost control over the interpretive process, a situation which could be rectified only through a reaccessing of a *single* meaning—that intended by the author. One effect of Schleiermacher's proposal was that subsequent interpretation would be largely characterized by the Protestant ideal of duty. The austerity of the task is reflected in the subtitle of Van Harvey's book, *The Historian and the Believer*, namely, *The Morality of Historical Knowledge. . . .* [4]

There was increasing suspicion in the nineteenth century that Schleiermacher's thesis was too psychologistic, that more attention ought to be given to the mutual life situation of author and exegete which makes understanding efficacious. This theory, developed by Wilhelm Dilthey and further enriched by the ideas of Kierkegaard and Heidegger, provided much of the thrust of the existentialistic hermeneutic which, though appreciative of certain necessary functions of historical criticism, felt compelled to add the dictum of Horace, recollected from Kierkegaard: *jam tua res agitur*—"this concerns you"! Bultmann's scholarship was a classic example of the residual respect historical-critical methodology enjoyed among those who questioned its omnicompetence. During that era historicism provided much of the raw material for Old and New Testament theologies of the *Heilsgeschichte* type, as well as some of the dynamic for the ill-fated "New Quest of the Historical Jesus"—however much its representatives argued otherwise. The celebrated "decline of biblical theology" was due in part to its ambivalence about historicism for it was unwilling either to abandon historicism

---

[4]Van A. Harvey, *The Historian and the Believer: The Morality of Historical Knowledge and Christian Belief* (New York: Macmillan Company, 1966).

or to accept it on its own terms. Rather than coming to terms with the problem of historicism biblical theologians turned to methodologies seemingly unplagued by the historicist issue, such as redaction criticism and literary techniques. While many of those engaged in redaction-critical scholarship were motivated by lingering historicist objectives and often interpreted their results and those of their colaborers as reconstructions of the theologies of "the Evangelists" rather than simply of "the Gospels," these self-interpretations were usually dismissed as idiosyncratic and irrelevant to the positive gains of this new type of scholarship. What was truly revolutionary about most redaction-critical studies was that the older question of "what really happened" was totally eclipsed by the focus *on the text*, as is readily apparent from the monographs of Willi Marxsen and Hans Conzelmann on Mark and Luke-Acts, respectively.

Literary criticism which today enjoys the highest respect among biblical scholars is conducted in virtual silence about historicist issues of earlier times. Textuality is the passionate concern of literary critics who see no need to raise historicist questions about biblical texts since such questions are not thought to be germane to such inquiry. Mythical narrative, dramatic narrative generally, and poetry do not raise such questions themselves and in the interest of rigor no attention is given to them. Whereas historicist scholarship stressed the "literal" meaning of the text, literary critics rightly suspect that the historicist approach illicitly differentiates between the "meaning" and the "text."

Meanwhile the discipline of philosophical hermeneutics has developed, primarily through the labors of Gadamer and Ricoeur, and has brought new anti-historicist options into the discussion. While I cannot in so brief an essay outline even the major insights of this epochal philosophical thinking, I should like to indicate that it has done much to bring textuality back into the center of hermeneutics and to replace the older moralistic notions of the role of the interpreter with a more proper emphasis upon aesthetic considerations, especially creativity. It is this latter approach which I should like to develop now, though the way I shall do so is largely of my own design.

Historicism fostered the notion that a text has one meaning, and that it is the moral task of the interpreter to single out that meaning. Schleiermacher's quest for the "mind of the author" was part and parcel of this moral ideal of *narrowing* the field of possible meanings to the "original" one. As we saw earlier, the role of the interpreter was viewed as under the moral mandate of this single meaning. Hermeneutical truth was said to have been achieved when the thinking of the subject corresponded to the thought of the object.

While this notion of the single objective meaning of the text receives enthusiastic support from both common sense and historicism, it fails to do justice to the aesthetic reality of "eminent literature" (Gadamer's term). When it is realized that what is to be interpreted ranks as a "literary creation," the recognition of the aesthetic reality of the text moves to the center of the discussion. Do creative works which win the respect of great cultures really have "one meaning"? I am reminded in this connection of Archibald MacLeish's famous line: "A poem should not mean / But be."[5] After years of professional identification with historicism, I have become committed to the idea that creative works achieve greatness more in terms of their power to *generate* meanings than in their success at *controlling* subsequent interpretations by an "original" meaning. Too long this expansive power of classics has been treated as an aberration to be remedied by the search for an original meaning! If my major assumption is trustworthy, it becomes the task of the interpreter to enter into this aesthetic process. The interpreter is to respond—creatively—to the meaning, not *behind* or *in* the work, but *of* the work. For the meaning of creative works is not detachable from their being; following MacLeish, I should say: their being *is* their meaning.

---

[5] Archibald MacLeish, "Ars Poetica," cited from *The Poet in America: 1650 to the Present*, ed. Albert Gelpi (Lexington MA: D. C. Heath and Company, 1973), 529.

We should not overlook the obvious fact that creative literary works, including those of scripture, have a definite specificity as well, that is, they are in some material sense *about* something rather than something else. This phenomenal feature of texts has played a determinative role in the interpretation of biblical texts, so determinate in fact that their meaning has been completely identified with their specificity. Literalistic and historicist interpretations make just such an identification. It should be apparent from what I have said earlier that I prefer to seek the intentionality of such texts in their textuality rather than in their specificity. This response would be an affirmation of the principle that the "meaning" and the "text" are not separate things, as historicism supposed. It would also be an affirmation that the "creativity" of the text should be responded to creatively, that is, imaginatively, rather than moralistically.

This imaginative approach to biblical interpretation has been a rarity in the post-Enlightenment period, and even modern redactional and literary studies do not fully represent it. Among the few true instances of such hermeneutical creativity as applied to biblical texts certain writings of Søren Kierkegaard stand out, the most notable being his interpretation of the story of "Abraham Sacrificing Isaac," narrated in Genesis 22. Modern commentaries on Genesis have approached this story with all the apparatus of historical-critical method and have produced some interesting "findings." One of these is that the story probably originated at a time when child sacrifice was common—possibly in the name of Jahweh—and was intended to make the point that Jahweh does not require—or no longer requires!—child sacrifices. A variation of this idea is that Israel's God, unlike the Canaanite deities, does not require child sacrifices. A second important suggestion from the critical commentaries is that the story is an etiological myth which grew up to "explain" an old local place name, "God-will-provide" (יהוה יִרְאֶה = Jehovah-Jireh), a suggestion strengthened by the fact that in the story there are three "puns" on the Hebrew word for "provide."

In these critical interpretations of the Sacrifice Saga based on the finest linguistic, archeological, and historical methods, important aspects of the text are noted, but in most cases we are left with only the vaguest notion as to how—to use Kierkegaard's borrowed phrase—"this concerns you." To be sure, "it concerns us" in the general way in which all biblical stories "concern us," but is there more to it than that?

Kierkegaard's interpretation of the Sacrifice Saga achieves this dimension of concern primarily by responding to it creatively. Rather than reducing the story to a "meaning," Kierkegaard, under the pseudonym of Johannes de Silentio, retells the story (for stories are to be retold) in four different ways, the important consequence being that the "interpretation" is itself "literary creation." This having been accomplished, he proceeds to meditate on the text; this meditation leads him to produce, not a "commentary" in the conventional sense, but a "Panegyric to Abraham." Abraham's dilemma, often overlooked in the critical commentaries, becomes Kierkegaard's dilemma. He wrestles with the story much as Jacob wrestled with God, and with the same consequence. Art gives birth to art in pathos. Through the free reign of the imagination Kierkegaard traced through every conceivable course of action open to Abraham—and to himself!—and showed that every one ends in paradox. Let us listen to two of them:

> If Abraham when he stood upon Mount Moriah had doubted, if he had gazed about him irresolutely, if before he drew the knife he had by chance discovered the ram, if God had permitted him to offer it instead of Isaac—then he would have betaken himself home, everything would have been the same, he has Sarah, he retained Isaac, and yet how changed! For his retreat would have been a flight, his salvation an accident, his reward dishonor, his future perhaps perdition.[6]

We see that his "interpretation" is not restrained by a single "orig-

---

[6]Søren Kierkegaard, *Fear and Trembling and The Sickness unto Death*, trans. Walter Lowrie (New York: Doubleday, 1954) 36-37; the work cited is "Fear and Trembling."

inal" meaning, but responds creatively to the story itself. The same is the case in the following (earlier) passage:

> If Abraham had doubted—then he would have done something else, something glorious; for how could Abraham do anything but what is great and glorious! He would have marched up to Mount Moriah, he would have cleft the fire-wood, lit the pyre, drawn the knife—he would have cried out to God, "Despise not this sacrifice, it is not the best thing I possess, that I know well, for what is an old man in comparison with the child of prom- ise, but it is the best I am able to give Thee. Let Isaac never come to know this, that he may console himself with his youth." He would have plunged the knife into his own breast. He would have been admired in the world, and his name would not have been forgotten; but it is one thing to be admired, and another to be the guiding star which saves the anguished. [7]

Kierkegaard's way of interpreting was a major influence upon existentialist hermeneutics, but the pathos deeply felt in the latter did not usually give birth to art. It creatively responded to the call that "the text concerns you," but the end product was mostly theory rather than literature.

I should like to conclude this hermeneutical essay by setting forth a theory of meaning drawn from Heidegger's ontological her- meneutics. Even though I develop my hermeneutical theories by ar- ticulating a hermeneutics of relationality and of Immediacy, I now turn to a Heideggerian idiom with the conviction that his approach and mine are not fundamentally dissimilar.

Eminent literature achieves its eminence from its "creativity." Its creativity derives from its nature as "disclosure," that is, as ἀλ- ήθεια—"truth" (= "unveiling"). This unveiling is a "letting be" of Being through creative textuality. Accordingly, interpretation should be—and only truly can be—a creative response to "disclo- sure" that is itself ἀλήθεια. This hermeneutical disclosure is not the guaranteed end product of the process of critical inquiry; it rather partakes of the nature of all creativity—it "occurs."

---

[7] Ibid., 35.

9 | Beyond Baur and Historicism

The critical issue to be addressed in this essay has long been a concern of mine: for fifteen years I approached the New Testament armed with the analytical techniques of historical-critical scholarship and the existentialist hermeneutics of Rudolf Bultmann. The former had the effect of "liberating" me from the oppression of the naive conservatism of my particular brand of Protestantism and the latter had the redeeming feature of ensuring that the text would continue to be my concern. The relationship of critical method and existential evaluation was as ambivalent in my career as in Bultmann's, but somehow by paying attention to both I was able to function in the guild with a good conscience. The most exciting aspect of New Testament study during those days was "New Testament Theology," a distinctive twentieth-century movement which met both my professional and personal religious needs. The uneasiness I experienced with Bultmann's negative attitude toward "Dogmatics" led me to a deep appreciation of Professor Fritz Buri's Existential Dogmatics worked out in conscious dependence upon Karl Jasper's Philosophy of the Encompassing.

After some time the Kantian commitments of Protestant theology in this century became exceedingly problematical for me, especially after serious attention to conceptual issues in physics convinced me that Kant's *Critique of Pure Reason* was deeply influenced by Newtonian physics. From this study of physics I developed a relational metaphysics which has the possibility of serving as a new paradigm for theology. In the course of this metaphysical endeavor—while still teaching New Testament—I became disaffected with many of my long-standing presuppositions for interpreting the New Testament. Not only had existentialism become a fading perspective in Western scholarship; biblical theology was also losing its appeal among younger scholars.

As I reassessed my role as an interpreter of the New Testament during those changing times, I felt that my relational schema could provide a worthy alternative to those priorities of my early career. I decided to retrace the course of development of modern biblical scholarship, and in doing so came to the conclusion that Rationalism—as the matrix of modern biblical scholarship—had stamped its image deeply upon those studies. This finding was important to me, for I had already determined that Rationalism was a truncated view of experience which had deeply—and adversely—affected Western modernity. Others were saying things similar: Hans Frei about biblical interpretation, and Michael Foucault about Western intellectual thinking. If such criticisms of Rationalism were valid, I thought, it might well prove to be the case that rationalistic biblical interpretation was the carrier of a set of commitments about reality which are questionable in the extreme.

Having been a demythologizer who felt that Bultmann's hermeneutical method freed the text from literalistic exegesis, I began to reassess his concept of myth. It became apparent to me that Bultmann's stated definition of myth, that is, "the representation of the other-worldly in terms of the this-worldly," was rationalistic—a fact evident in his negation of ancient cosmology as "prescientific" (that is, unscientific") and of biblical notions of deity as "anthropo-morphic." I hasten to say that Bultmann's program of existentializ-ing the meaning of the New Testament was based, not upon his stated definition, but upon its converse to which I can subscribe, namely, "the representation of the this-worldly in terms of the other-worldly." Given this fact, there is no great gulf between his understanding of the intentionality of the text and my own, except that I have abandoned his existentialist idiom for a relational one.

My hermeneutic theory focuses on the intentionality of narra-tive texts of eminent literature, but can be generalized to include other literature within the same ambience. To the contrary, Ration-alism founded itself on a negation of myth, and its progeny—histor-ical-critical method—shared in this negation. As a force behind the nineteenth-century Quest of the Historical Jesus, Rationalism pro-moted such negation as a means to determine the salvageable "his-torical truth" obscured in narrative myth. "Historical truth" became the goal of the quest, so that the measure of a text's worth was judged to be the degree to which "what actually happened" could be discerned in it by rational method. The *conditio sine qua non* of Ra-tionalism was its separation of "myth" from "truth," and its sub-sequent denigration of the former by the latter. Rationalism separated *logos* (λόγος) from *mythos* (μῦθος), and defined the for-mer as *ratio*; it was but one step further to identify *mythos* with *pseudos* (ψεῦδος). Only *logos* as *ratio* could be *alētheia* (ἀλήθεια). While narrative myth could not—*ex hypothesi*—be "true," it was thought to provide some access to the historical reality which the mythical narrative poorly represented. Thus arose the rationalistic notion of the truth-*behind*-the-text, a notion which serves as a foun-dation of historicism. Historical reconstruction was its goal, and critical methodology its means. It was a corollary of historicism that narrative texts of eminent literature ought to be judged primarily in terms of their success at representing the past. That is to say, since narrative texts *pretend* historical representation, their failure to do so accurately brings them under the charge of being "tenden-tious"—a term made famous by Ferdinand Christian Baur with respect to the Acts of the Apostles. By the "making and testing of hypotheses"—to use Schweitzer's phrase—rationalistic historical criticism claimed to be able to determine "historical fact" through the application of critical methodology to "reports" which manifest varying degrees of trustworthiness. Since Rationalism had established itself by exposing many historical "frauds," such as the Donation of Constantine, it was impelled to extend this "hermeneutics of suspicion" (to use Ricoeur's phrase) to all narrative texts of eminent literature.

At this point I should like to set forth and criticize three objections to such historicism as applied to mythical narrative, and then to suggest alternative principles for dealing with it.

(1) Historicist hermeneutics negates the text rather than "letting it be"; this it accomplishes by instrumentalizing it for a purpose it was never designed to serve. Metaphysically stated, historicist hermeneutics transfigures the Immediacy of Textuality into the mediateness of an *organon*.

(2) Historicist hermeneutics transforms the aesthetic Immediacy of the text—its textuality—into the issue of the morality of the historian-author of the text. Fundamental to such hermeneutics is the notion—as formulated by Van Harvey—of "The Morality of Historical Knowledge." In my opinion, such moralism arises not out of narrative textuality, but out of rationalistic modernity.

(3) Historicism imposes on mythical narrative an *alien* intentionality and then faults the text for failing to yield what is expected of it.

Already apparent in these objections are certain positive principles underlying an alternative hermeneutic. Some of these principles can be stated as follows:

(1) The reality of texts of eminent literature is precisely their *textuality*. The clue to their intention lies therefore in aesthetic rather than historicist considerations. I shall say more about this principle later.

(2) The task of hermeneutics is to enter into the "givenness" of the text—into what it *makes present*—rather than setting this aside

to search for what is not "given" or present in the text, namely, for an absent Past which, according to rationalistic historicists, the text pretends to represent. In accord with this claim I am here advocating a hermeneutics of Immediacy, thus calling upon a term which I find fully commensurate with the notion of relationality.

(3) What mythical texts intend, that is, what they "let be," is the imaging of experience as relatedness. They achieve this in narrative form by "*character*-izing" experience, that is, by forming it into functional roles, into *personae*. From a relational standpoint it is a distortion of the intentionality of such dramatic format to suppose that the "characters" are being *posited* as entities, whether human or divine. The question of the entitivity of the separate characters is not within the horizon of mythical texts. No one steps forward—"out of character," as it were—to say that the story is really true or that the characters really exist *a se*. Since such questions lie outside the scope of mythical narrative, to pursue them through the text by rationalistic means leads inevitably to some degree of negation of such texts.

The relational theory respects the limits of mythic narrativity. The text is assumed therein to be an inviolate whole whose integrity is to be respected. Like every classic aesthetic work the text manifests its creativity in its power to generate congruent meanings, whereas moralistic theories of interpretation, such as historicism, presuppose the text to have one meaning which controls the process of interpretation. In historicist hermeneutics the "being" of the text, respected in relational hermeneutics, is transformed into a heuristic function of value to the historian.

These general hermeneutical considerations are applicable to the Book of the Acts of the Apostles. An ever so brief summary of Acts-criticism should illustrate the abuse which the book has suffered.

In his epochal commentary on Acts, Ernest Haenchen presents a taxonomy of opinions which can be useful for our purposes: scholars have assumed that the special and unique character of the Acts is a consequence of either (1) the author's ignorance of what really transpired in the first Christian century, or (2) of his willful intention to deviate from the true course of events for some special purpose. Haenchen observes that the former assumption led to Source Criticism, the latter to Tendency Criticism.

What we notice initially about late eighteenth- and early nineteenth-century Acts-criticism is the isolation of the Book of the Acts from the Gospel of Luke, a move which brings into being what we call "Acts-criticism," that is, a special branch of New Testament scholarship relatively independent from other types of inquiry, such as Gospel Research. Only with the emergence of redaction criticism of Luke-Acts in the 1950s did this phenomenon come to an end. In retrospect we could say that the analytic approach to the New Testament created a "separate entity"—the Acts—and then speculated about its attributes. According to precritical and redaction critical views, no such "separate entity" existed; the real entity is "Luke-Acts." We have before us a prime example of the vagaries of analytic method and its tendency to create its own conceptual entities. A comparable case in astronomy occurred in the 1960s with the realization that it is more responsible to think of the real entity under scrutiny in geophysics as the Earth-Moon system rather than the Earth *a se.* My fundamental metaphysical position is that everything is a function of everything else, so that synthetic assumptions are more faithful to reality than analytic ones.

In any event, from about 1840 to 1950 there did exist a discipline of Acts-criticism which by its own ground rules followed a predictable course. During that period the central issue was the comparison of the primitive church and the Apostles Peter and Paul as set forth respectively in the Acts and the Pauline Epistles, and the creation of hypotheses to explain the disparities. Baur's bold thesis of open hostility between the Apostle Paul and the Jewish Christians (including the Twelve) enjoyed wide acceptance in the nineteenth century and continues to shape opinions today. In two rather distinct phases Source Criticism served both to "explain" the discord between the Acts and the Pauline Epistles and to "defend" the author of Acts against the charge of willful distortion of the events of the Apostolic Age. The latter phase, largely remembered for the work of the great historian Adolf von Harnack, was mainly a response to the theories generated by the Tübingen School.

The nineteenth century was the age of historicism par excellence, a fact due in large measure to the shadow which Hegel cast over that century. Two scholars who are credited with the greatest initiative in bringing historicist criticism to the New Testament are Ferdinand Christian Baur and his one-time student, David Friedrich Strauss. Schweitzer has conditioned us to think of Strauss primarily as a historian—one who introduced scholarly sophistication into the Quest of the Historical Jesus—but later in this paper I shall try to set Strauss's work in a different perspective. In order to do so, I must first come to terms with Baur.

Baur—called by Peter Hodgson "the Father of Modern Historical Theology"—was probably the first biblical scholar in whom rationalism was rather fully translated into historicism. Sharing something of Hegel's conceptual visions—although the degree to which he is indebted to Hegel is debated—Baur pursued a course of rigorous historicism. As a historian deeply moved by philosophical considerations, Baur was an apologist for a distinctive point of view with respect to the character of Christianity, a fact which goes a long way toward explaining why he was more of a critic of "bad" documents than a reconstructor of the "true" chronology of the ancient Church. His main purpose—evident in his philosophical writings—was to show the superiority of Pauline, that is, Gentile, Christianity over any and all types of Petrine, that is, Jewish, Christianity. For Baur, Pauline Christianity was the first and only true type, and the attempt of the author of the Acts to indicate the contrary was his mortal malady.

Baur shared with the rationalistic historians the conviction that the Acts should have been a reliable record, and even *pretended* to be. It was this assumption that generated his use of the moralistic term, "tendentious," to describe the character of the Acts. For, in Baur's view, no narrative author—even of a New Testament writing—is worthy of respect who alters the true course of events for a-historical purposes, and especially if these purposes entail the (mis)representation of the earliest Christian community—which he held a priori to be Gentile—as Judaistic. It is important to add that I am not now arguing that the Acts *is* a good historical source. I am only trying to demonstrate the way in which the historicist question leads away from the text by misconstruing its intentionality.

The great work on the Acts by Foakes-Jackson, Lake, and their colaborers was a brilliant continuation of historicist scholarship, for it still treated the Acts as a "special entity" (though Cadbury was less guilty); it sought the analogues to the author in *historical* writings of antiquity; and, finally, it was unperceptive to new directions in biblical scholarship which were beginning to spell the end of historicism.

The real pioneer in this era was Martin Dibelius whose essays on Acts helped to bring about the later focus on redaction and literary criticism. When Vielhauer opened the new era of Luke-Acts criticism with his essay on Paulinisms in Acts, he was deeply indebted to Dibelius, as was—less consciously—Hans Conzelmann. The virtue of this approach was its restoration—without protest!—of the unity of Luke-Acts, and its lack of concern with historicist questions. The redaction critics had made a quantum leap in the direction of *letting the text be*, for they often concluded their work without stating any opinion about the "historicity" of the events. Redaction criticism thus served to undermine "historicism" and its "quest" mentality. It would have survived to enjoy long-lasting respect, had it not been for its own conceptual problematic, namely, its ill-fated dependence upon the short-lived movement of biblical theology; for the latter was too time- and culture-bound to commend itself for very long.

It was redaction criticism's close relation with literary criticism that would prove to be more significant, for literary criticism and its cognates rapidly became the favored methodology among the younger scholars who work primarily with the text. In literary criticism—as opposed to redactional—aesthetic rather than material and historicist priorities obtain. Structural features of the text, which were *functionally* important to the redaction critics, become *essentially* significant to the literary critics. Granted that much literary criticism is wanton, its assumption of the fundamentality of textuality is an abiding hermeneutical insight. In the hands of ontologists like Heidegger and Gadamer it has become something of a new horizion for modernity. *Textuality* shares in the reality of *Sprachlichkeit,* and *narrativity*—of prime importance to interpreters of the Gospels and the Acts—is but a dramatic instantiation of textuality. With these claims we are at the threshold of a revolution in modern self-understanding whose far-reaching implications can be but dimly seen.

Now to return to the New Testament text per se. Two major writings in the New Testament canon have suffered most at the hands of historicist critics: the Gospel of John and the Acts of the Apostles. Their narrativity suggested to historicists that their intention should have been to record. When extensive comparisons with the other Gospels and the Pauline Epistles, respectively, generated major discrepancies between the "accounts," the Fourth Gospel and the Acts were discredited by those with singularly historicist priorities. The reversal of this negation occurred in separate, but related moves: Eduard Reuss and Baron von Hügel in the nineteenth century asserted the unique philosophical character of the Gospel of John, and Dibelius and the redaction critics in the twentieth century laid claim to the positive theological character of Luke-Acts. A further mandate urging itself upon us is to generalize these earlier insights in the direction of a hermeneutics informed principally by recognition of the nature of mythic narrativity, for this is a phenomenon at the heart of originative religious literature. Such hermeneutical theorizing should be a conscious philosophic undertaking, especially in view of the ill effects of a century and a half of ontological abuse of the text.

Earlier I promised to give an interpretation of Strauss different from those which have usually prevailed. Ever since the time Schweitzer highlighted Strauss as the first truly critical voice in the Quest of the Historical Jesus, it has been customary to regard him as a historian in the rationalist tradition. With few exceptions—Karl Barth being the most notable—Strauss has continued to be interpreted in this way. I should like to suggest alternatively that Strauss—in composing the first edition of his *Life of Jesus Critically Examined*—was seeking primarily to make a contribution to hermeneutics rather than to historicism. He consciously rejected both supernaturalism and Rationalism, and presented in their place a theory of mythic narrativity. Many modern interpreters of Strauss have failed to grasp this fact, and have thus faulted him for his largely negative contribution to the recovery of the "historical Jesus." The reason no satisfactory residual portrait of the historical Jesus is to be found in the first edition is—as Barth claims—that Strauss had no such end in view. If Strauss is to be remembered as anything more than just another rationalist, it will be because we begin to see his initial project in the light in which he placed it. Strauss's insight into the character of the gospels as mythic narrativity was a positive judment of the first magnitude, and—as far as the first and fourth editions are concerned—was the singular aim which guided his inquiry into the nature of the Gospels.

This revision in the usual evaluation of Strauss has important consequences for understanding the character of the Book of Acts. Strauss's harshest critic was his close friend and former teacher, Baur, who faulted him on two counts: (1) Strauss had focused on the individual units of synoptic material without giving attention to the intentions of their several authors; and (2) Strauss's failure to focus on the writings rather than the separate stories meant that he had no valid *modus operandi* for making certain judgments about "concrete historical truth." Subsequent scholarship has shown the validity of Baur's first objection and I should not want to defend Strauss against Baur on this point. But on the second point the matter is quite different: Baur simply failed to grasp the true goal of Strauss's edition of 1835. A summary of Baur's position will illustrate my contention:

> The "firm ground of concrete historical truth" is first attained by establishing a critical perspective on the writings, from the basis of which

the historicity of individual pericopes can be evaluated. Such a perspective, according to Baur, represents a genuinely "historical understanding" of the Gospels; any other procedure is abstract, negative, or dialectical.[1]

We have seen all too well what happens to the quest for the "perspective" of the writings at the hands of Baur. Hodgson admits that Baur's overemphasis upon tendency criticism was a reaction to Strauss's more fragmented approach. Whatever Strauss's shortcomings in the first edition, his failure fully to grasp Baur's criticism and positive suggestions was not a defect; in striking upon the "mythic character of the text" of the Gospels—and by extension, of the Acts—Strauss made a hermeneutical discovery of greater intrinsic worth than Baur's historicism. Baur had been led by his rationalistic historicism to negate the Book of Acts; his otherwise defensible insight into the perspective of the writings became for him a tool of rationalistic negation, a consequence—as I have tried to show—of his conceptual denigration of Judaism and Petrine Christianity. For what Baur meant by authorial perspective was—if we may judge from his conclusions about the Acts—the "historical dependability" of those who wrote in the form of narrative. Strauss's intention was so far removed from Baur's that the attempt of the former to rectify later editions so as to conform to more acceptable tastes, met with failure as well. In the fourth and final edition he reverted to the pristine position of the first.

If we abandon completely Baur's theory as he presented it, we move toward an understanding of the Acts that is more in accord with its intention—intention now being understood, not as "the mind of the author" (another discredited notion), but as the character of its textuality, namely, mythic narrativity. With the redaction critics we forsake the historicist goal in order to *let the text be*. It is not the case that we are without precedent in this task, for—as I have indicated—the redaction critics performed this task rather

---

[1]David Friedrich Strauss, *The Life of Jesus Critically Examined,* ed. Peter C. Hodgson, trans. George Eliot, The Life of Jesus Series, ed. Leander E. Keck (Philadelphia: Fortress Press, 1972) xxix.

well. Nevertheless, they left the task incomplete because they focused on the character of particular books per se, the result being a kind of "theological individualism"—as Hugh Anderson called it. Without discrediting the positive gains of the redaction critics, I should like to suggest that the hermeneutical task needs to be further generalized before seeking to interpret works of mythic narrativity, such as the Acts. Such a hermeneutic would be based on a deep understanding of the nature of mythic narrativity through its shared phenomenality with similar texts of eminent literature.

I cannot claim to have undertaken this task on a broad scale with respect to the Acts, but I venture to suggest some guidelines for those who may wish to do so.

(1) *Formal considerations should replace material ones,* if we are to avoid many of the pitfalls of the past. Notions like "a canon within the canon," which accounted for Baur's negation of the Acts, result from making *material* considerations primary. When Baur's critics—like the late Johannes Munck, for example—have sought to defend the Acts for its material worth, they have in fact operated from within Baur's historicist hermeneutics.

I want to suggest that when *formal* considerations replace material ones, the true religious character of the work can be seen. Dogmatic debates appealing to ideas *within* the text assume its material features to be fundamental. When, to the contrary, fundamentality is reserved for formal features of the text, such narratives bear witness mythically, that is, formally and generically, to what is fundamental about experience. The *material* argument within mythic narrative is the ground of its specificity and particularity, so that whatever insights arise therefrom are local and parochial. Its *formal* character—to the contrary—opens the reader out onto the universally religious. Although from a relational perspective it is questionable to build ontologies on its *material* elements, it is fully appropriate—and deeply so—to build an ontology on its *formal* character as mythic narrative. The clue to such an ontology would lie in its functional characterization of relations, since relations are fundamental. Differently expressed: relatedness is fundamental.

(2) *Intrinsic considerations should take precedence over extrinsic ones.* By this I mean that the penetration of the phenomenality of mythic narrativity should rank above comparisons with similar and dissimilar documents. We know that when extrinsic procedures have prevailed, negation of whole texts has been the result. Such was the case with the Acts at the hands of Baur and the historicists. Nevertheless, these analytic treatments of texts have enjoyed wide scholarly recognition and may have some secondary residual role in the hermeneutical task, but they do not foster religious awareness as much as they may serve to sharpen doctrinal debate.

It is of interest that, even judged on material grounds, the case of the historicist against the Acts is beginning to weaken. Here I refer to Krister Stendahl's relatively new theory of the central meaning of the Apostle Paul's thought. If Stendahl is correct in maintaining that the center of Paul's message is *vocation* rather than *justification*—and I am inclined to agree with him against centuries of Augustinian-Lutheran interpretation (which includes Baur!)— then the great discrepancy between the Acts and the Pauline Epistles turns out to be an apparition. We could then safely conclude that the bias against the Acts of the Apostles had been the result of an unholy alliance between historicism and Lutheran dogma. I am willing to grant that the whole issue is more complex than these sharply stated charges indicate; nevertheless, they have sufficient cogency to awaken us from our historicist slumber.

The Acts must be seen in a way radically different from previous viewpoints. The new way could turn out to be identical or similar to the relational approach I have outlined. However that may be, the fundamental role which the Scriptures have played in the Church has insured the centrality of hermeneutics in the Church's life and thought. In my understanding, it is the *being* of the text that must be the basis of a valid hermeneutics; too long—and with deleterious effects—*aspects of* the text rather than the *text* per se have been made central. In the case of texts such as the Gospels and the Acts, their *being* is mythic narrativity—a mode of textuality uniquely suited to image reality as relatedness.

10 | A Metaphysics of the Relational Self and Its Theological Implications

In view of my intention to develop a relational theory of the self in the wider context of both Eastern and Western Christian thought, I shall need to give more attention to theological issues than was the case in my previous writings.

The particular approach which I have chosen for this purpose lends itself to the following progression of subtopics:

- The Metaphysical Accountability of Theology
- Selfhood as a Theological and Metaphysical Issue
- A Metaphysical Theory of the Relational Self
- Theological Implications.

In developing this theme I shall attempt fairly to represent both Eastern and Western Christian thought, since I consider the future well-being of modern culture to rest on a synthesis of these grand traditions.

The Metaphysical Accountability of Theology

In a rare tribute, the great Anglo-American metaphysician, Alfred North Whitehead, wrote in 1925: "Greece is the Mother of Europe"[1]; and in 1919: "The safest characterization of the European philosophical tradition is that it consists of a series of footnotes to Plato."[2] As Whitehead was fully aware, these insights are as applicable to theology as to philosophy; for after the period of Late Antiquity, philosophy survived in a theological form, namely, as Christian philosophy. The emergence of Christian theology represented—in Harnack's famous phrase—"the acute Hellenization of dogma." While Harnack viewed the phenomenon as adventitious and negative, my understanding of the nature of theology leads me to judge it as necessary and positive. For both historically and thematically, philosophy and *a fortiori*, metaphysics, belong not only to the *bene esse* of theology, but to its very *esse*. That this is so attests to the seriousness and perennial significance of theology, for theology in its metaphysical role provides the interface between Tradition (ἡ παράδοσις) and culture, between the *Visio Dei* and the *Visio Mundi*, between Church and Academy, and (*pace* Tertullian) between Jerusalem and Athens!

The interface of which I speak is no fixed boundary between two static entities; for Tradition is "living" and thus open rather than closed to its cultural environment, while culture constantly changes in response to challenges from within and without. The very existence of theology is the basis for the possibility of the perennial relevance of Tradition for culture; indeed, it is a principal manifestation of that relevance itself.

---

[1]Alfred North Whitehead, *Science and the Modern World, Lowell Lectures 1925* (New York: The Free Press, 1967 ed.) 7.

[2]Alfred North Whitehead, *Process and Reality: An Essay in Cosmology*, corrected edition, ed. David Ray Griffin and Donald W. Sherburne (New York: The Free Press, 1978) 39.

During the thousand years or more of Christian philosophy, the important legacy of philosophic thought shaped Christian thought from within. The basic questions of theology assumed the shape of philosophic issues, however much their resolution may have rested upon the triumph of Tradition. Christian theologians, whether Eastern or Western, mediated disputes over rival traditions by translating them into philosophic choices. The theologians kept the philosophical legacy alive by their persistent efforts to make their theological positions metaphysically accountable. The language of Tradition was—as we say today—polyvalent; its "surplus of meaning," to use Paul Ricoeur's phrase, had the effect of generating rival interpretations, so that Tradition could not be appealed to *alone* to settle such debates. With great philosophical acumen, theologians evaluated alternate readings of the Tradition as choices between fundamental philosophic positions. This is not to say that the resolutions of the great theological debates, such as Christology or Iconoclasm, were purely philosophical. Rather, the disputes had the redeeming effect of drawing attention to the fundamentality of the Tradition. By the dialectic of dispute and philosophic mediation, the fundamental character of the Tradition was brought to self-consciousness. Tradition proved itself to have a disciplined character; its "rightness" as "teaching" (ὀρθο-δοξία) was the judgment that it faithfully *images* reality. This judgment has been uniquely challenged in the West where the "hermeneutics of suspicion" (Ricoeur's phrase, again), as developed, say, by Feuerbach and Freud, is the ominous legacy of the Enlightenment. The gradual reversal of this devaluation of religious experience and language in this decade is attended by a new sense of the metaphysical depths of traditions. Hermeneutics and Ontology dominate the present discussion of religious tradition(s), as is evident in the writings of Hans-Georg Gadamer, Paul Ricoeur, Mircea Eliade, Raimundo Panikkar, and others. In the wake of this important work, the metaphysical accountability of theology through the centuries is becoming more widely recognized.

The rise of the modern world out of medieval Christian culture was attended, and possibly caused, by philosophy's declaration of independence from theology. Just as during and after the Greek Enlightenment, philosophy developed as a quasi-secularized discipline, so after the Western Enlightenment, philosophy has evolved out of its own agenda. That the break with theology was gradual attests to the philosophical integrity of Christian theology through the centuries. But the fact remains that the role and task of the modern theologian is different because of the independent status of philosophy in the modern world. Faced with an enormous range of philosophical positions, the contemporary theologian—in order to make the Tradition relevant—must choose between them or synthesize his own philosophical position. Western theologians have in fact followed one or the other of these courses of action, defending their decisions by complex arguments. In fact, theologians have restated the Tradition under the strict conditions of many different philosophical systems: existentialism, Kantianism, Neo-Kantianism, analytic philosophy, Marxist philosophy, process philosophy, and Neo-Hegelianism—to name only the principal ones. Other theologians have viewed this conscious dependence of theology upon given philosophic systems as the introduction of alien elements into the faith; those who have turned to available philosophic systems to explicate the faith regard those who resist doing so as victims of theolog*ism*.

My perception is that the vitality of theology down through the centuries has derived from its openness to philosophic inquiry. In the discussion of the question of selfhood which follows, I hope to demonstrate anew the theological relevance of the philosophical investigation of experience. I shall begin this project by developing a transitional theme:

Selfhood as a Theological and Metaphysical Issue

In view of what I have said about the healthy interaction between philosophy and theology, it will be apparent that I cannot keep the two entirely separate in my development of this phase of my essay, Nevertheless, I shall attempt to do so to the extent that it is possible.

Affirmations about the nature of selfhood, or personhood, appear in all traditions. Myth and Ritual reflect the self-perceptions of the cultures which nurtured them. There is at least this much truth in Feuerbach's judgment that "Theology is Anthropology." Ancient cosmologies mirror the personal values and expected social roles of their devotees, as do modern cosmologies. No "reductionism" is intended by this claim; for I hold that the only way to describe the meaning of selfhood is in "relation," that is, relationally: in-relation-to-the other, in-relation-to-the cosmos, in-relation-to-the-Eminent-Other. Myth and Ritual express this truth by dramatization, by "character-ization," that is, by depicting "characters-in-relation." Tradition transmits this insight into the relational character of reality to later generations; theology mediates the alienation from Tradition of later generations brought about by change of circumstance.

Religion images its cosmology; philosophy articulates its worldview. The imaging endemic to religion gives birth to aesthetic creation in the form of icons of varying magnitude; philosophy regenerates itself in dialogue and self-criticism. Each in different ways represents human affirmation: religion, in the form of symbols; philosophy, in the form of systems. Both are affairs of the human spirit, of the person.

Judeo-Christianity shows no interest early on in what God is apart from human relatedness. All the attributes of God are relational. Personhood is set forth relationally. To explicate the biblical sense of ὁ θεός (God) is to explore the deep mysteries of the "*pro nobis*"; to explicate the biblical sense of personhood is to explore the manifold characterizations of "*coram Deo*." This imaged mutuality of God and person was so fundamental to the Tradition that no *kataphatic* manner of speaking of God was judged to be religious; the *apophatic* tradition, by eschewing the Promethean attitude in theology, preserved the deep insight that the Eminent Other is not Wholly Other. I am aware that the quintessence of apophatic theology has never been articulated in just this way, but I offer it for your examination. The lesson I draw from this observation is that at the heart of Tradition the issue of selfhood is inseparable from the issue of Divinity.

Contrary to popular opinion, the issue of selfhood in philosophy is not genetically independent of its role in religion. The recognizable form in which the issue of selfhood has dominated the history of Western philosophy can be traced uniquely to Socrates, whose understanding of the task of the philosopher, γνῶθι σαυτόν, derived not from his philosophical forebears or contemporaries, but from the Portal of the Sanctuary of Apollo at Delphi, the heart of the indigenous religion of Greece! While far too little is known to determine the specific role which that inscribed message played in Olympian religion, the fact remains that Western philosophy cannot claim that its preoccupation with self-knowledge represents a complete departure from religious insight.

But it was a departure nonetheless. It signalled the birth of relentless inquiry, and, by implication, of a new kind of self: one whose very nature was to be a *seeker*, an iconoclast of partial truths, and whose destiny was to become a ready prey for those who think of Tradition as closed, rather than open. Martyrdom was the "seed," not only of the Church, but of Socratic Philosophy.

Unlike Tradition, philosophy in its critical function *tests* rather than *testifies*; it turns every answer into a question. Throughout the history of Western philosophy no answer has remained sacrosanct—whether of religion or of philosophy itself! The most persisent message of philosophy is that all attempts to state truth mirror the humanity of those who make such attempts. Even so, this need not be a counsel of despair. For philosophy has also developed a synthetic function, whereby diverse and seemingly unrelated aspects of experience are shown to form larger wholes. In its constructive task, namely as metaphysics, philosophy has sought to bring all of experience under one rubric. There is a tendency to judge such vast speculative schemes as transexperiential; I prefer to regard them as schemata of experience. Such schematizations are as much *in-*

ner, as they are *outer*, charts of reality. There is great wisdom in Hegel's fusion of *inner* and *outer*.

Western religious philosophy synthesized a view of the self out of classical, Roman, and Near Eastern traditions. Augustine's *Confessions* signalled the arrival of a new *psyche*, a new selfhood in Western consciousness. Although he thought of it as Pauline, some contemporary scholars, notable among whom is the Swedish-born American theologian Krister Stendahl,[3] judge the "plagued conscience" of Augustinian theology to be a true emergent, a new phenomenon in the history of Western culture, a mutation of that psyche delivered over to the West by the earliest Tradition. The fact that no true analogues to "the introspective conscience of the West" are to be found in Eastern Christianity supports the thesis that it is a mutation formed in the West. The Reformation, for all its novelty, gave a new importance to the introspective psyche and, by institutionalizing it, laid the foundations for the secularized individualism of the West. The stage was thus set for the bold philosophic innovation which gives modern philosophy its most distinctive character, namely, Descartes's positing of the fundamentality of the "subject-self." Modern Subjectivity was born, and at that historic moment, something ancient and venerable died. The extraction of the "subject," that is, the *Cogito*, by means of Methodic Doubt created the dilemma of the metaphysical status of the "object," that is, the *Cogitatum*. Kant's *Critique of Pure Reason*, which was written to deal with this dilemma, has been said, by Heidegger, to have as its "metaphysical center" the problem of "the objectivity of the object."[4] Kant's conception of the central problematic of experience became determinative for the subsequent history of Protestant,

---

[3]Krister Stendahl, "Paul and the Introspective Conscience of the West," an essay in his book, *Paul among Jews and Gentiles* (Philadelphia: Fortress Press, 1976).

[4]Martin Heidegger, *What is a Thing?*, trans. W. B. Barton, Jr. and Vera Deutsch, with an analysis by Eugene T. Gendlin, Gateway edition (Chicago: Henry Regnery Co., 1967) 55-56.

and most recently of Catholic, theology. Personhood conceived as subjectivity has been the prevailing paradigm of Western culture; individualism, its prevailing psychosocial manifestation. This phenomenon is, in my opinion, the fundamental issue underlying the major ideological differences between East and West.

Selfhood, or personhood, in the Orthodox Tradition is different from that of the Western Augustinian legacy which defined both Roman Catholic and Protestant traditions, as the special terms Deification (ἡ θέωσις), Synergy (ἡ συνεργία), and the cognates Christ-Bearer (χριστοφόρος) and Spirit-Bearer (πνευματοφόρος), richly indicate. In these notions, as in others developed in Patrisic Theology, Personhood is perceived *manifestationally*, that is, in the strict context of the mystery of the Trinity. The Trinitarian doctrine was carefully guarded, for with its distortion, selfhood would be distorted. The mystery of the Trinity discloses the mystery of personhood to be *incarnational, spiritual, mystical, relational*. In the words of a former colleague of mine, "it is man's true destiny to share by grace in all that which the Holy Trinity possesses by nature."[5] This colleague, Dr. Angelos J. Philippou, contrasts the Orthodox emphasis with the Western in the following way:

> While the West, from St. Augustine onwards, has been chiefly preoccupied with what is in *man* which allows him to receive God, eastern theology is concerned mainly with establishing what is in *God* which makes Him able to give Himself to man. This difference is of the greatest significance.

---

[5]Angelos J. Philippou, "The Mystery of Pentecost," in the volume he edited: *The Orthodox Ethos: Essays in Honor of the Centenary of the Greek Orthodox Archdiocese of North and South America* (Oxford: Holywell Press, 1964) 91. Philippou's statement is based on St. Maximus's famous remark: "man 'becomes by participation (μεθέξει) that which the Archetype is as cause' (κατ' αἰτίαν or φύσει)" (Maximus, *Opusc. theol. et pol.*, P. G. XCL, 33C; I have cited this quotation from John Meyendorff's *A Study of Gregory Palamas*, trans. George Lawrence, [The Faith Press, 1964] 2nd ed., 175, and n. 78.   .

[6]Ibid., 94.

I cannot—nor would it be necessary to do so in this setting—fully develop the principal aspects of the great legacy of Orthodox anthropology signalled by the previously mentioned comprehensive notions. What strikes a Westerner as most distinctive in the great Orthodox heritage is that personhood is viewed *elpidically*, rather than *mnemonically* (compare the contrast between ἡ ἐλπίς [= hope] and ἡ μνημοσύνη [= memory] in the next section). Professor Nikos A. Nissiotis, in the volume edited by Dr. Philippou, succinctly states this distinctive emphasis as follows: "For Orthodoxy, man is not defined by what he is but by what he can become in drawing near to his archetype, the icon of his *imago* which is Christ." The clear contrast with the West is more emphatic in an amplification he subsequently provides: "Man, then, is not to be defined by his sin, by his state of bondage, but in relation to his end in Christ and the work of the Paraclete in him."[7] I have long thought that the difference between Orthodox and Western notions of experience is most graphically represented by the contrast between the *Pietà* on the one hand, and the *Christus Victor* of the Orthodox Easter Iconograph on the other. The *Pietà* is *descensional*; the Easter Iconograph, *ascensional*. And, while in Philippians 2 these notions are presented as inseparable aspects of one truth, the Orthodox emphasis is more faithful to the *telic* or *eschatological* affirmation of reality portrayed in the scripture passage. In view of this claim, I count it somewhat ironic that Philippians 2:5-11 is uniformly referred to in the West as the *fons et origo* of "kenotic Christology"; perhaps we should begin to view it as a manifesto of *"anastasial* Christology"* (from the Greek, ἡ ἀνάστασις = resurrection).

I shall return to several of these themes in the last part of this essay after setting forth my relational theory of selfhood. In previous publications I have given priority to showing that my relational theory is consonant with the views of a few Western and of many Far Eastern thinkers. I shall not repeat that discussion here, except

---

[7]Nikos A. Nissiotis, "The Importance of the Doctrine of the Trinity for Church Life and Theology," in *The Orthodox Ethos*, 60.

in the case of Meister Eckhart, who deserves special consideration for reasons which I hope will become apparent.

A Metaphysical Theory of the Relational Self

Previously I spoke of the critical and synthetic tasks of metaphysics. It is to the latter that I now turn as a means of setting forth a view of selfhood rigorously derived from experience. My hope is to articulate a coherent and comprehensive view of the self which will avoid the Scylla of Subjectivism and the Charybdis of Objectivism.

To the extent that experience presents itself to us apart from existing conceptualizations, it shows itself to be a unity. It is only when we reflect upon it that it bifurcates into a host of multiplicities, such as subject-and-objects, prior and posterior, mind and brain, *Cogito* and *Cogitata*. In my opinion, the limited options of Idealism and Realism arose from the practice of ontologizing, that is, concretizing, certain of these abstractions. Such abstractions are useful for certain purposes, but prove to be misleading when turned into fundamental notions.

Although experience manifests certain temporal and spatial features, it cannot be said from a relational point of view, to be "located in space and time." In the West, particularly, the notion of the self has been radically temporalized and spatialized, with dire consequences for morality and psychology. It is altogether possible that the "plagued conscience" of the West arose uniquely out of the Augustinian tendency to "temporalize the will," that is, to separate Act from Intention. The Western theologian who reacted most strongly against this transformation of the Christian psyche was Meister Eckhart. The essence of his position is best represented in the title assigned to one of his sermons by its translator into English: "Get Beyond Time!"[8] The beginning of this sermon is the *locus classicus*

---

[8]Raymond Bernard Blakney, *Meister Eckhart, A Modern Translation*, Harper Torchbooks edition (New York: Harper & Row, Publishers, 1941) 212.

for Meister Eckhart's distinctive notion of temporality, and the following excerpt from it captures its essence.

> There is the soul's day and God's day. A day, whether six or seven ago, or more than six thousand years ago, is just as near to the present as yesterday. Why? Because all time is contained in the present Now-moment. Time comes of the revolution of the heavens and day began with the first revolution. The soul's day falls within this time and consists of the natural light in which things are seen. God's day, however is the complete day, comprising both day and night. It is the real Now-moment, which for the soul is eternity's day.[9]

This notion of temporality is at the heart of Meister Eckhart's controversial interpretation of the Logion: Μακάριοι οἱ πτωχοὶ τῷ πνεύματι (Matthew 5:3). Meister Eckhart shows us that all moral injunctions lapse into contradicion if selfhood is conceived as "located in space and time."

Metaphysics, both critically and synthetically, is preoccupied primarily with the problem of entitivity, or to use Heidegger's classic formulation, with *Die Frage nach dem Ding*.[10] I very often rephrase this question as follows: what is truly fundamental and belongs to the characterization of any possible state of affairs? The whole of human history is dotted with rival answers to this question. My judgment about many of these answers is that they finally fail to be fundamental, in that, upon rigorous inspection, they prove to be further reducible.

The predicative character of Western languages has done much to lead us astray, metaphysically. We create our reality out of the structured components of our language, that is to say, out of its subjects and objects. The "subjects" and "objects" seem invariant; their relationships, infinitely variable. With the invention of certain formal operations, like Cartesian Methodic Doubt, it is but a small step toward making either the subject, or the object in some philosophies,

---

[9]Ibid.

[10]Heidegger, *What is a Thing?*

the single invariant. In the former case, we have Idealism; in the latter, Realism.

To avoid these perils of one-sidedness, it will be necessary to overcome the dilemma of polarity which they force upon us. I should like to suggest that the possibility of doing so lies in a reconsideration of the character of action itself. Prior to its reflective bifurcation into subject and object, the act is unitary. Without the elaborate tools of reflection, it is the *acting* that presents itself. Using conventional symbolism, we can express this acting as *a*-related-to-*b*, or *aRb*. Western philosophy has given priority to the *relata*, that is, the subject or the objects, rather than to the *relatio*. Relational metaphysics, to the contrary, affirms the fundamentality of *relatio*, the relation, the *relating*. Thus it maintains the coherence, or better, the co*in*herence, of the act. *Per definitionem*, there can be no actor (agent) or thing-acted-upon *prior* to the acting (*actio*). Every attempt to posit them outside the act fails, because we can do so only by appeal to other acts where the same restrictions obtain.

The *relata*, from which our notions of subject and object derive, I prefer to think of as derivatives, as useful abstrations. They are, indeed, to be regarded as co-derivatives, in that they emerge co-ordinately in reflection upon experience. In reflection dual aspects of the action emerge, a subjectival and an objectival. They so emerge, not because they exist prior to the reflection, but because reflection imposes the structure of thinking consciousness (that is, *cogito* and *cogitatum*) upon experience.[11] Reflective thinking is analytic, and so "divides in order to conquer." Indeed, it can be said that consciousness creates its entities in its own image.

Western metaphysics has tended principally to ontologize the *relata* associated with subjectivity, namely, the ego, the *cogito*, consciousness, the subject, the "I." Western culture has institutional-

---

[11]The Swiss theologian, Fritz Buri, has devoted considerable attention to this "structure of thinking consciousness" as the starting-point for theological reflection: cf. his *Denkender Glaube* (1966; English translation, 1968); *Wie können wir heute noch verantwortlich von Gott reden?* (1967; English Translation, 1968).

ized this subjectivity into individualism. It is no wonder that the Christian teaching on "self-denial" has never been fully intelligible to the Western mind. Against the background of temporalized Augustinian selfhood, that fundamental insight into the nature of self has foundered on the rocks of egocentricity; for "self-denial" has been too easily turned into "self-assertion." As long as the "denying of self" is understood as the *act* of the *agent*-self, that is, the subject, the result will take one of two forms: to the extent that the agent-self regards the attempt at self-denial to have succeeded, the Moral Ego will be the result; to the extent that the agent-self regards the attempt to have failed, the result will be the "plagued conscience" of which I have already spoken. More than any other Western writer, Meister Eckhart fathomed the mystery of self-denial and rendered it intelligible. The essence of his teaching is elegantly and concisely stated by D. T. Suzuki:

> Our spiritual discipline . . . consists not in getting rid of the self but in realizing that there is no such existence from the first. The realization means being "poor" in spirit. "Being poor" does not mean "becoming poor"; "being poor" means to be from the very beginning not in possession of anything, and not giving away what one has. Nothing to gain, nothing to lose; nothing to give, nothing to take; to be just so, and yet to be rich in inexhaustible possibilities. . . . To be absolutely nothing is to be everything.[12]

Suzuki's statement surfaced in the context of a dialogue with Father Thomas Merton, whose life was a struggle to clarify and exemplify this spiritual truth. As a Westerner, Merton realized how utterly strange the self-effacing acts of such Christian ascetics as the Desert Fathers appeared to the Western mind. Their deep perception of the enigma of the *ego* is evident in Merton's comment:

> [The Desert Father] could not dare risk attachment to his own ego, or the dangerous ecstacy of self-will. He could not retain the slightest identification with his superficial, transient, self-constructed self. He had

---

[12]D. T. Suzuki, "Wisdom in Emptiness" published in Thomas Merton, *Zen and the Birds of Appetite* (1968) 109.

to lose himself in the inner, hidden reality of a self that was transcendent, mysterious, half-known, and lost in Christ.[13]

The Desert Fathers remind us by their lives that self-denial is not finally a theoretical problem, but a task.

The notion of selfhood which discloses itself intuitively rather that reflectively is that of the *relational self*. In relational selfhood there is no "I" separated from a "Thou"; for the "experiential other" signals not "separation," but "mutuality." The very being of the "I" of "I-Thou" is a co-being. Accordingly, it is more faithful to experience to say that the "I" is created by the relation than to say that the "I" creates the relation through its prior subjectivity. The "I" emerges with its "Thou" in the same creative act. Reality thus discloses itself relationally as "mutuality."

This notion of the relational self is not a form of Personalism, for the "Thou," that is, the "experiential other," is not necessarily personal in the usual sense of that term. From a relational perspective, the difference between "other persons" and "other things" is not based on a prior distinction between "mutuality" and "non-mutuality," for relational thought can assign no meaning to "non-mutuality." Indeed, the difference does not finally rest on the nature of the object, for then we should be thrown back upon a subject-object paradigm of experience. The difference between "other *persons*" and "other *things*" must reside in the nature of the relating, that is in the verb. The "experiential other" yields the co-derivative "other *person*" if the action entails *full mutuality*; it yields the co-derivative "other *thing*" if the action entails *restricted mutuality*.

The metaphysics of the relational self is thus distinguished by the threefold claim that

1. experience is a unity
2. mutuality is reality

---

[13]*The Wisdom of the Desert: Sayings from the Desert Fathers of the Fourth Century*, trans. Thomas Merton (London: Hollis and Carter, 1961) Introduction, 7.

3. distinctions within this unity are rational constructs, that is, abstractions.

My judgment is that all three claims necessarily follow when experience is examined synthetically rather than analytically.

Theological Implications

It is my conviction that the synthetic approach to selfhood characteristic of this relational metaphysic manifests an *apophatic* respect for the mystery of personhood, whereas the analytic approach appears to be *kataphatic*. For "mystery" does not denote some inherent irrationality in the object, whether the Trinity or the self; rather it announces the denial of self-sufficiency before the final realities. The lesson from this is that the term "religious" properly describes an *act*, a posture, a "relationship to," rather than some quality in the thing itself. Religion is *praxis* before it is *theoria*.

Throughout this essay I have stated certain theological implications of the relational theory of selfhood where it seemed appropriate to do so. There is one aspect of the subject, however, which has been only intimated by the symbolic designation, "the Eminent Other." This symbol emerges from the examination of Tradition in terms of a relational hermeneutics. Tradition originates in Myth and Ritual which take the form, as a rule, of dramatic or narrative enactment. In such contexts ὁ Θεός (God) appears as a "character-in-relation," as do the persons who additionally comprise the *dramatis personae*. ῾Ο Θεός is unfolded, as are the persons, in a dramatic way, that is, relationally. The story shows no interest in what the "characters" may be outside the narrative, for narrative is a strict genre allowing no one to "step out of character." It is this feature, more than any other, which accounts for the suitability of narrative as a form of religious affirmation. It cannot assign any meaning to what is outside its narrative world; thus it is complete in itself. This claim does not require us to think of ὁ Θεός as a character like the others. To the contrary, ὁ Θεός is represented as "the

Eminent Other." But "Eminent Other" does not mean "Wholly Other," for "other"—from a relational perspective—necessarily entails "mutuality." The religious character of the narrative does not derive from a portrayal of "Eminence" as what is least mutual among the characters, but rather as what is paradigmatically mutual. The mutuality developed in characterization belongs to the genius of narrative; the religious narrative seeks to establish that "mutuality" is reality. This it accomplishes aesthetically and religiously, that is, by imaging relatedness "eminently." That all stories do so to some degree belongs to the genre. The archetypal character of religious narratives lying at the source of the Tradition derives from their pure portrayal of "relatedness" as the final reality.

Ὁ Θεός is the "Eminent Other," "the Holy Other." These descriptive characterizations do not arise from a consideration of God as Divine Object, as some theologians suppose; for, from a relational perspective every subject is a subject-object, and every object an object-subject. They arise, rather, from the special character of certain verbs. For it is a special kind of *relating* that is religious, and not the *relatum*. Such verbs, or actions, as "worshiping," "praying," "praising," "sacrificing," uniquely represent religious *praxis*. One of the great truths of our Tradition is that devotion to an object—even to one considered Divine—is not worship, but idolatry. I can best express my central claim by adapting the subtitle of an article which I came across last year in a professional art journal:[14]

To the non-religious, the term "God" is a noun;
To the religious, God is a verb.

We should not conclude from this statement that the difference between the nonreligious and the religious is *merely* verbal. What it affirms is quite the contrary: the difference between "nonreligious"

---

[14]Adapted from the article by S. H. McGarry on "Gary Moss," in *Southwest Art* (November 1980): 67.

and "religious" is the difference between unreality and reality. It is the difference between idolatry and worship, between self-assertion and self-denial, between life and death.

Bibliography

A. Books

Barrett, William, editor. *Zen Buddhism. Selected Writings of D. T. Suzuki.* Anchor Books edition. New York: Doubleday, 1956.

Barth, Karl. *Protestant Thought: From Rousseau to Ritschl.* New York: Harper & Brothers, 1959.

Bertocci, Peter A. *The Person God Is.* The Muirhead Library of Philosophy. London: Allen & Unwin/New York: Humanities Press, 1970.

Blakney, Raymond Bernhard, editor. *Meister Eckhart. A Modern Translation.* Harper Torchbooks edition. New York: Harper & Row, 1941.

Blanshard, Brand. *The Nature of Thought.* New York: Macmillan Co., 1940.

Bradley, F. H. *Appearance and Reality.* Oxford: Clarendon Press, 1893.

Buri, Fritz. *Denkender Glaube.* Bern: Verlag Paul Haupt, 1967. ET: *Thinking Faith: Steps on the Way to a Philosophical Theology.* Translated by Harold H. Oliver. Philadelphia: Fortress Press, 1967.

_____. *Wie können wir heute noch verantwortlich von Gott reden?* Tübingen: J. C. B. Mohr, 1967. ET: *How Can We Still Speak Responsibly of God?* Translated by Charley Hardwick and Harold H. Oliver. Philadelphia: Fortress Press, 1968.

Cassirer, Ernst. *Substance and Function and Einstein's Theory of Relativity.* New York: Dover Publications, Inc., 1953.

Feuerbach, Ludwig. *Über Spiritualismus und Materialismus besonders in Beziehung auf die Willensfreiheit.* Gesammelte Werke. Edited by W. Schuffenhauer. Volume 11: Kleinere Schriften, IV: 1861-1866.

Flew, Antony, and Alasdair MacIntyre, editors. *New Essays in Philosophical Theology.* The Library of Philosophy and Theology. London: SCM Press, 1955.

Frei, Hans. *The Eclipse of Biblical Narrative: A Study in Eighteenth and Nineteenth Century Hermeneutics.* New Haven: Yale University Press, 1980.

Gadamer, Hans-Georg. *Truth and Method.* A Continuum Book. New York: The Seabury Press, 1975. First German edition, 1960; 2nd. ed., 1965.

Hartshorne, Charles. *Creative Synthesis and Philosophic Method.* London: SCM Press, 1970.

_____. *The Divine Relativity: A Social Conception of God.* New Haven: Yale University Press, 1964.

_____. *Man's Vision of God and The Logic of Theism.* New York: Harper & Row, 1953; first published in 1941.

Harvey, Van A. *The Historian and the Believer: The Morality of Historical Knowledge and Christian Belief.* New York: Macmillan Co., 1966.

Heidegger, Martin. *Being and Time.* Translated by John Macquarrie and Edward Robinson. New York: Harper & Brothers, 1962. First German edition, 1927.

_____. *What is a Thing?* Translated by W. B. Barton, Jr. and Vera Deutsch, with an analysis by Eugene T. Gendlin. Gateway edition. Chicago: Henry Regnery Co., 1967.

Herrigel, Eugen. *Zen in the Art of Archery.* With an introduction by D. T. Suzuki. Translated by R. F. C. Hull. Vintage Book edition. New York: Random House, 1971.

Jaspers, Karl. *Der philosophische Glaube angesichts der Offenbarung.* Munich: R. Piper & Co. Verlag, 1962.

Kierkegaard, Søren. *Fear and Trembling and The Sickness unto Death*. Translated by Walter Lowrie. New York: Doubleday, 1954.

Kümmel, Werner Georg. *The New Testament: A History of the Investigation of Its Problems*. Translated by S. McLean Gilmour and Howard C. Kee. Nashville: Abingdon Press, 1972.

Laszlo, Ervin. *Introduction to Systems Philosophy. Toward a New Paradigm of Contemporary Thought*. Harper Torchbooks edition. New York: Harper and Row, 1972.

Merton, Thomas. *Zen and the Birds of Appetite*. New York: New Directions, 1968.

Meyendorff, John. *A Study of Gregory Palamas*. Translated by George Lawrence. Second edition. London: The Faith Press, 1964.

Moore, G. E. *Philosophical Studies*. Totowa NJ: Littlefield, Adams & Co., 1968; first published in 1922.

Nishida, Kitaro. *A Study of Good*. Trans. V. H. Viglielmo. Tokyo: Printing Bureau, Japanese Government, 1960; first published in 1911.

Oliver, Harold H. *A Relational Metaphysic*. Studies in Philosophy and Religion 4. The Hague: Martinus Nijhoff Publishers, 1981.

Perrin, Norman. *Rediscovering the Teachings of Jesus*. New York: Harper and Row, 1967.

Philippou, Angelos J. *The Orthodox Ethos: Essays in Honor of the Centenary of the Greek Orthodox Archdiocese of North and South America*. Oxford: Holywell Press, 1964.

Popper, Karl R. *The Logic of Scientific Discovery*. Revised edition. London: Hutchinson, 1968.

Russell, Bertrand. *Philosophical Essays*. New York: Simon and Shuster, 1966; first published in 1910.

_____. *Principles of Mathematics*. Second edition, reprint edition. New York: W. W. Norton & Co., Inc. [n.d.].

Schweitzer, Albert. *The Quest of the Historical Jesus: A Critical Study of Its Progress from Reimarus to Wrede*. New York: Macmillan Co., 1950 edition.

Stendahl, Krister. *Paul among Jews and Gentiles and Other Essays*. Philadelphia: Fortress Press, 1976.

Strauss, David Friedrich. *The Life of Jesus Critically Examined*. Edited by Peter C. Hodgson. Translated by George Eliot. The Life of Jesus Series, edited by Leander E. Keck. Philadelphia: Fortress Press, 1972.

Torrance, Thomas F. *Space, Time and Incarnation*. London: Oxford University Press, 1969.

————. *Theological Science*. London: Oxford University Press, 1969.

Whitehead, Alfred North. *Process and Reality: An Essay in Cosmology*. New York: Harper Torchbooks edition, 1960; first published in 1929.

————. *Process and Reality: An Essay in Cosmology*. Corrected edition, edited by David Ray Griffin and Donald Sherburne. New York: The Free Press, 1978.

————. *Science and the Modern World, Lowell Lectures 1925*. New York: The Free Press, 1967; first published in 1925.

The Wisdom of the Desert: Sayings from the Desert Fathers of the Fourth Century. Translated by Thomas Merton. London: Hollis and Carter, 1961.

B. Articles

Barr, James. "Story and History in Biblical Theology." *Journal of Religion* 56 (1976): 1-17.

Bedau, Hugo Adam. "Complementarity and the Relation between Science and Religion." *Zygon* 9 (1974): 202-24.

Blanshard, Brand. "Internal Relations and their Importance to Philosophy." *Review of Metaphysics* 21 (1967): 227-36.

Bultmann, Rudolf. "The New Testament and Mythology." *Kerygma and Myth* I. Edited by Hans Werner Bartsch. London: S.P.C.K., 1953; first published in 1941. Pages 1-44.

Cobb, John. "Buddhist Emptiness and the Christian God." *Journal of the American Academy of Religion* 45 (1977): 11-25.

Harvey, Van. A. "D. F. Strauss' *Life of Jesus* Revisited." *Church History* 30 (1961): 191-211.

Jaspers, Karl. "Myth and Religion." In *Kerygma and Myth* II. Edited by Hans Werner Bartsch. London: S.P.C.K., 1962; first German edition, 1948. Pages 133ff., 143-44.

McGarry, S. H. "Gary Moss." *Southwest Art* (November 1980): 66-77.

McKay, D. M. " 'Complementarity' in Scientific and Religious Thinking." *Zygon* 9 (1974): 225-44.

MacLeish, Archibald. "Arts Poetica." in *The Poet in America: 1650 to the Present*. Edited by Albert Gelpi. Lexington MA: D. C. Heath and Company, 1973. Page 529.

Oliver, Harold H. "Hope and Knowledge: The Epistemic Status of Religious Language." *Cultural Hermeneutics* 2 (1974): 75-88.

Schlegel, Richard. "Quantum Physics and Human Purpose." *Zygon* 8 (1973): 200-20.

Wisdom, John. "Gods," *Proceedings of the Aristotelian Society* (1944). Reprinted in *Philosophy and Psychoanalysis*. New York: Philosophical Library, 1953. Pages 149-68.

Index

A. Names

B. Subjects